P9-AQE-067

Let Freedom Ring

A 40-Day Tactical Training for
Freedom from the Devil

**FR. JAMES ALTMAN
FR. RICHARD HEILMAN
FR. WILLIAM PECKMAN**

Imprimatur, Madisoniae, die XV Ianuarii, MMXI, Jacobus Robertus Bartylla, Vicarius Generalis Dioecesis Madisonensis

The imprimatur is not an indication of agreement or endorsement but only a statement that the work is free of error in the realm of doctrine concerning faith or morals as proposed by the magisterium.

Nihil Obstat, die XV Ianuarii, MMXXI, Timotheus Cavanaugh, Censor Deputatus

Copyright 2021 By Fr. Richard Heilman

All rights reserved.
First Edition, 2021

978-1-7365190-0-4

MATER
MEDIA

MaterMedia.org

For Our Savior Jesus Christ, who by His Passion, Death, and Resurrection has given us the ability to share in the conquering of the demonic; the Sacraments as avenues of grace to do battle; His Mother, the Most Holy Queen of the Angels, to come to our defenses; the angelic Host under the great St. Michael to combat the wickedness and snares of the devil; and the great cloud of witnesses, the saints, as our fellow combatants and protectors.

Through Christ and the Heavenly Court, we never enter the battlefield alone.

THE COVER, UNCOVERED

By FR. RICHARD HEILMAN

Before we begin, I wanted to take a moment to discuss the meaningful cover of this book. You will notice that the design contains a statue of St. Michael the Archangel with an American flag and a "Christmas Star" gleaming in the background. Each has a special connection to our current events and the purpose of this training.

The American flag represents our current call as Americans to combat evil and fight for God's truth. Who would have ever thought that the same loss of freedoms experienced due to socialism would be felt across America in the year 2020? People never would have willingly given up their rights prior to the spread of Covid-19; however, when their businesses were shut down and their health and lives appeared to be at risk, they believed those in power had their best interests in mind. That's when the government stepped in and we the people found ourselves being conditioned to depend on (and be controlled by) those in power. This simply cannot stand in the land of the free and home of the brave!

The statue of St. Michael the Archangel is the same one that is in Rome on top of Castel Sant'Angelo, known as "The Castle of the Holy Angel," and it has quite the story behind it. Around 590, toward the beginning of Pope St. Gregory the Great's papacy, there was a terrible plague where many were dying. During this time, the Pope would tirelessly process through the city with incense while prayers were being recited. During one such procession, the plague was lifted as an image of the Blessed Mary Ever Virgin was carried through the streets. In the book *The Golden Legend: Readings on the Saints*, Jacobus de Voragine describes the event, saying "The poisonous uncleanness of the air yielded to the image as if fleeing from it and being unable to withstand its presence: the passage of the picture brought a wonderful serenity and purity in the air." Then the pope saw an angel of the Lord standing on top of the castle of Crescentius, wiping and sheathing a bloody sword. This miraculous event marked the end of the plague; the castle was renamed in the angel's honor, and a statue of St. Michael the Archangel was placed on top to signify his protection over the city. This statue was chosen for the cover to represent our collective call to God to give us a similar blessing. We are asking Him to put an end to this plague and to protect us from the mounting religious oppression we face.

The star signifies our hope in the midst of darkness. It represents a celestial event that occurred on the winter solstice in 2020. After facing a "Goliath" plague of evil all year, we were gifted with a rare (occurring only every 800 years) conjunction of Jupiter and Saturn. This resulted in a bright light to behold on the darkest day of the year, just four days before Christmas - our very own "Christmas Star." After a year where evil had done all it could to instill fear, God deemed to grant us a gift of hope right before we celebrated the birth of our Savior, Jesus Christ. We discerned that God was revealing His Presence while reminding us to remain hopeful because, "It is always darkest before the dawn." In John's Gospel, Jesus says, "I have come into the world as a light, so that no one who believes in me should stay in darkness" (John 12:46).

By participating in this 40-day training we, the "children of light," are combating evil. Looking at the cover reminds us that we are fighting for freedom and His truth; asking for a miraculous end to the plagues we face; and choosing to see the light in the midst of darkness, through our hope in Jesus Christ.

Contents

INTRODUCTION
By FR. WILLIAM PECKMAN

In 1969, singer/songwriter John Fogerty wrote the song, "Bad Moon Rising." The late 1960s were a trying time for the citizens of the United States. They were in the midst of a horribly unpopular war in Vietnam; the sexual revolution had upended the traditional understandings of human sexuality, marriage, and family life; the country had just gotten over a contentious and violent election in 1968; and domestic terrorism was rising and would come to a head with the "Days of Rage" in October of 1969. It felt like the U.S.A. was selling its soul and trouble was coming. In the Church, the tsunami called "the Spirit of Vatican II" washed over the horizon nearly destroying all it touched. Seminaries and convents emptied out, and priests left by the droves. The shift within liturgy was just starting to rear its head and confusion reigned. Indeed, a bad moon was rising.

In the year 2020, there began a similar ominous threat. Again, we find ourselves in violent times. We find horrible confusion in our churches and our societies. The world has plummeted into a pandemic which has become so politicized that one can scarcely glean what is true and what is false. American politics, normally a blood-sport in the best of times, has become a *Mad Max* style Thunderdome in which everyone chants, "Two candidates enter, one candidate leaves." The Church's leadership has floundered under the weight of two decades of scandal, that seem to have no end. We are seeing a vocation crisis and continued contraction of Catholic life, Catholic identity, and Catholic institutions. Belief in the most basic teachings of the Church dwindle, such as the Real Presence in the Eucharist, and the best our leadership can do is say they will make a brochure about it. A bad moon rises again.

John Fogerty wrote the song "Bad Moon Rising" after watching the movie *The Devil and Daniel Webster*. In the story, a luckless New Hampshire farmer, Jabez Stone, sells his soul to the devil for a combined ten years of good fortune. When the devil comes to collect his prize after ten years, the farmer hires the famed jurist and politician, Daniel Webster, to defend him.

If you take a minute to look around, it appears that we are now the ones in need of defense. The bad moon has returned, and this time the devil is coming for more than the farmer. Today, he is preying with the full power of the demonic upon a people who have largely dropped their weapons. There is no Daniel Webster to plead our cause in this story; instead, we must turn to our true champion to beat back the demonic: Jesus Christ.

Looking for the Devouring Lion

In I Peter 5:8, we read, "Be sober and watch: because your adversary the devil, as a roaring lion, goeth about seeking whom he may devour." Most of us have seen nature shows. One of the more tense moments is when predators start to circle a herd. They look for stragglers, the young, and the sick first; these members make for an easy kill. A big enough pride of lions can decimate a herd, especially if they have unfettered access — when shepherds abandon their flocks, it is only a matter of time.

As the smoke cleared to reveal the widespread damage of the "Spirit of Vatican II," one of the casualties was the change in how the Church addressed the demonic. The *Rituale Romanum*, the book containing the formulas for blessings, gave way to the *Book of Blessings*. Emptied from the *Rituale* were the prayers of exorcism over things. In fact, the blessings of things also diminished in favor of prayers to bless the people who owned them. Popular spirituality downplayed, or even eliminated, the sense of the demonic in favor of a "let's circle up, hold hands, and sing" mentality that largely did away with the transcendent altogether. The idea of spiritual warfare, spiritual armor, and being watchful of the devil fell by the wayside and became the purview of fundamentalist Protestants. The devil became a caricature and the stuff of entertainment. In our arrogance we thought we could dismiss the devil and demonic to the realm of mythology and hence they would magically go away. They didn't. They won't.

The devil, he who divides, is still prowling with stunning accuracy. He has picked off a good part of the herd. Sixty-five percent of Catholics don't go to Mass on a regular basis. Seventy percent do not believe in the Real Presence of Christ in the Eucharist. And the numbers go even lower regarding Confession. We are dropping our strongest weapons against the devil, leaving him almost total unfettered access to our flock — the Church.

Standing Behind the Lion of Judah

At no juncture though, are we without hope. Jesus Christ, the Lion of Judah, is willing to stand between His flock and the devil. We must make a fundamental choice. Which side of the Lion of Judah will we be on? This book is an exercise in standing behind the Lion of Judah. To be behind Him means to follow Him. It means to change our lives to be in union with His will.

What has gotten us to this point is our insistence on walking apart from Jesus. This was facilitated by engaging in the madness of trying to mold a faith, a religion, a relationship, and a Messiah to be comfortable and easy. The resulting false Messiah is little more than a cardboard cutout, a cheap facsimile that does not fool the devil for a moment. To fall in line with Jesus, His armies, and His heavenly court requires us to take up our armor. The goal of these 40 days of prayer, fasting, and abstinence is to rejoin the battle with Christ in the lead.

In the Gospel of Mark, Chapter 9, Jesus is transfigured. Coming down from the Mount of the Transfiguration, He encounters a kerfuffle arising from a demonic presence that the apostles are unable cast out. After Jesus finishes the job, He tells them that some demons can only be cast out through prayer and fasting. With this knowledge in mind, we must address the current demonic influence in our society through prayer, fasting, and abstinence. In this book, we lay out 40 ways the demonic distort the truth, enslave us to sin, and wedge themselves into the relationships we are called to have as adopted sons and daughters, through Jesus Christ, with God our Father. In these 40 days we will align ourselves, by the grace of God, with the Lion of Judah — the Good Shepherd who defends His flock.

The Regimen

Any army must have a regimen of training that hones their minds, bodies, and souls into warriors; otherwise, the soldiers would get mowed down by a professional enemy. This 40-day training contains elements for all three parts of our beings to keep us an integrated whole, focused on the battle. Each day will be broken into prayer, reflection, and reparation, and contains elements designed to strengthen our spiritual, physical, and mental selves. In doing this, we offer no quarter for the devil to find lodging.

Each day you will be provided with a checklist to help you stay on track. Here is an overview of the training protocol:

Opening Prayer:
Before reading the day's material, pray the Prayer for Freedom from the Devil (pg. 255)

Reflection: Read the daily reflection, written by one of the three authors, on a particular manifestation of the demonic and the sin it leads to. Familiarize yourself with the corresponding virtue and plan of action to cultivate.

Prayers: Pray the reparation and exorcism prayers related to the manifestation of the day. Then follow them with a daily litany (pg.256-273):

Monday: Litany of Humility
Tuesday: Litany of St. Michael the Archangel
Wednesday: Litany of St. Joseph
Thursday: Litany of the Most Precious Blood of Jesus
Friday: Litany of the Sacred Heart of Jesus
Saturday: Litany of the Immaculate Heart of Mary
Sunday: Litany of the Blessed Sacrament

Acts of Reparation and Penance: Incorporate the following acts of reparation and penance into your day/week. They are designed to hone your mental, physical, and spiritual lives. Consider them a gym.

- ❖ Pray a Rosary daily - with the intention of exorcising the manifestation discussed that day.
- ❖ Pray a Divine Mercy Chaplet daily - in reparation for the sin caused by the manifestation of the day
- ❖ Do either a spiritual or corporal work of mercy (for someone you have harmed through your sin or someone who has harmed you through theirs).

14

❖ Fast or abstain as prescribed by your designated level (see Levels section below)

❖ Exercise for a prescribed time, based on your ability/level (see Levels section below)

❖ Go to confession once a week (where available).

❖ Refrain from all use of conventional media throughout the 40 days, and limit one's use of social media to one hour a day for non-business or evangelical use.

Levels

The fasting, abstinence, and exercise components of this training will be divided into four levels. All levels commit to the acts of reflection and prayer discussed previously. Remember, the Rosary and Divine Mercy Chaplet can be recited while exercising!

Understanding that age, ability, and health are factors, determine the level that is the best fit for you:

White Level: Recommended for pregnant women, senior citizens, and those with serious medical conditions.

Red Level: Recommended for those who do not think they can do the blue level.

Blue level: Recommended for those called to go "All In!"

Black level: For clerics.

Level	Fasting/Abstinence Regimen	Daily Exercise Regimen
White	No fasting. Abstain 3x a week from sweets, soda, junk food, and fast food	Exercise for 30 min. + Spiritual reading for 30 min.
Red	Fast on Wednesdays and Fridays. Abstain from sweets, soda, junk food, and fast food the 5 other days of the week	60 min.
Blue	Fast 3x a week (on Wednesdays, Fridays, and any another day except Sunday) Abstain from sweets, soda, junk food, and fast food for all 40 days	60 min.
Black	Fast 3x per week (unless age or medical conditions are an issue) Abstain from sweets, soda, junk food, and fast food for all 40 days **See note for clerics below!**	60 min. (30 min. for those over 65 or who have medical conditions)

*Note for Clerics

In addition, clerics are asked to do the following:

- Commit to Holy Hour every day (prayer, reflection, and some acts of reparation can be done during this time).
- Make more time for the confessional and daily Mass.
- Pray all hours of the Divine Office daily for 40 days.
- Commit to confession once a week.
- In a special way, offer the prayers for those placed under your pastoral care and do your acts of reparation for those harmed by the actions of any cleric, including yourself.

These 40 days cannot be a one and done activity. Our prayer, devotion, and sacrifice must be as relentless as the opponent we fight. We need to take back the ground we have lost. The demons do not stay because of their power alone, they stay by invitation or indifference on behalf of the possessed and influenced.

Day 1

Freedom from FEAR

By FR. WILLIAM PECKMAN

In the Garden of Eden, the devil tempts Adam and Eve. He lies to them. His lie is effective because it taps into fear. The fear is simple: God does not want what is good for you. The devil sells a fear to Adam and Eve that God

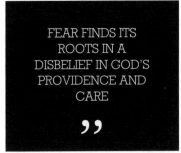

FEAR FINDS ITS ROOTS IN A DISBELIEF IN GOD'S PROVIDENCE AND CARE

wishes them to be perpetually ignorant of good and evil (even though they already knew the good), and that they are missing out without that knowledge. Fear finds its roots in a disbelief in God's providence and care. God knows this and, in the Scriptures, He tells us repeatedly to not be afraid. Overcoming fear is trusting in God.

Fear rules our nation now. It used to be that the American Dream was the ability to act rightly and freely and set a course independent of one's socioeconomic status. In the last 100 years the American Dream transformed into accumulation of possessions and status. Now the American dream has turned into a nightmare of anarchy by which the dream is complete autonomy and self-determination independent of God, science, or reason. The fear comes from a belief that this life is all that there is, and we must create a reality conducive to our personal truth. Anyone who challenges this is to be feared and despised.

Fear rules within most churches now too. It has reduced the evangelical call of the Great Commission to a call for the comfortable and non-challenging. It has stilled our tongues on moral issues, gutted our catechesis, emptied our seminaries, and decimated the priesthood. Being Catholic has always carried a stigma in this country. With the scandals in the Church, fear of being accused of things one would never do is a strong deterrent to answering God's call. It was for me. When the purveyors of fear have raised their voices, we Catholics have allowed ours to be scared silent. A fearful person who will not stand up against the lies of a human being will never stand up to the lies perpetrated by the father of lies, the devil. We would do well to heed Jesus' rebuke of His apostles in Matthew 8:26, "Why are you fearful, ye of little faith?" He says this as they are being tossed on the sea by a strong storm.

It might be said that courage is the virtue that combats fear. It goes deeper. The real virtue to cultivate is the theological virtue of faith. To countermand the devil's use of fear (that God does not want what is good for us or will abandon us if we follow Him), we must develop faith. Faith makes us able, and willing, to put our trust in His goodness and plan.

Because it is a theological virtue, the virtue only grows with the assistance of the grace of God. We will not be able to cultivate faith without the sacramental life of the

Church. Even when circumstances prevent our participation in the sacramental life of the Church, the fervent desire to participate in the sacramental life of the Church allows that opening for God to flood us with the grace to grow our faith. Such desire has aided the imprisoned, the ill, and the exiled.

Faith must lead to conversion. If not, then the grace of God is squandered. We shall have to answer for this. Conversion is an outward and inward sign of the trust and faith we have in God. Conversion sets the devil on his heels. It calls out his lie. Faith will lead us to a place where we can stand out against the rising tide and fight against the diabolical. Dead men float downstream, weak men are pushed downstream, but strong men can walk against the current and move forward. Faith is the powertrain to give us such abilities.

Prayer of Reparation

My Lord and my God, we have allowed the temptation of the devil to move our hearts to doubt in Your goodness. We have stilled our tongues in the face of evil. We have been too fearful to stand out in our culture, allowing the strong storms to quell our trust in You. In our fear, we have allowed the ancient foe to advance. We turn to You Lord, in our sorrow and guilt, and beg Your forgiveness for our fear and timidity. We beg for the grace of Your goodness to build up within us what You sought to build up in Your apostles in that tempest-tossed boat. We know, Lord, if You will it, it will be done. Trusting in you, we offer our prayer to You who live and reign forever and ever. Amen.

Prayer of Exorcism

Lord God of heaven and earth, in Your power and goodness You created all things. You set a path for us to walk on and a way to an eternal relationship. By the strength of Your arm and Word of Your mouth, cast from Your Holy Church every fearful deceit of the devil. Drive from us manifestations of the demonic that oppress us and beckon us to faithlessness and fear. Still the lying tongue of the devil and his forces so that we may act freely and faithfully to Your will. Send Your holy angels to cast out all influence that the demonic entities in charge of fear have planted in Your Church. Free us, our families, our parish, our diocese, and our country from all trickery and deceit perpetrated by the devil and his hellish legions. Trusting in Your goodness Lord, we know if You will it, it will be done, in unity with Your Son and the Holy Spirit, one God, forever and ever. Amen.

🔔 DAY 1 CHECKLIST 🔔

__ Prayer for Freedom from the Devil - pg. 255

__ Daily reflection and prayers

__ Litany of the day – pg. 256

__ Pray a Rosary (intention: exorcism of fear) – pg.275

__ Divine Mercy Chaplet (in reparation for: sin due to fear) – pg. 279

__ Spiritual or corporal work of mercy (see pg. 254)

__ Fast/abstain (according to level)

__ Exercise (according to level/ability)

__ Refrain from conventional media (only 1 hr. of social)

__ Examination of conscience (confession 1x this week)

Day 2

Freedom from DESPAIR

By FR. RICHARD HEILMAN

There is a stirring scene in the sixth chapter of John's Gospel, a chapter referred to as the "Bread of Life Discourse." Jesus had just told the crowd, "Whoever eats my flesh and drinks my blood has eternal life." The response by nearly all was, "This is a hard teaching. Who can accept it?" Jesus returns with, "The Spirit gives life; the flesh counts for nothing." And then, in the 66th verse of chapter 6 of John's Gospel, or rather John 6:66, almost everyone leaves: "From this time many of his disciples turned back and no longer followed him."

The crowd who abandoned Jesus had abandoned hope. They despaired. So, what did they do? They turned back to the emptiness of merely existing in the flesh. This emptiness, or desolation, is the place the devil wants us to be. It is Satan's kingdom.

I believe it is no accident that the chapter and verse of this act of despair in John's Gospel is 666. We are given free will. We can choose God or not. In the Book of Revelation, 666 is the number of the beast or the number of man. Once separated from God, Satan wants us to believe we are merely one animal (beast) among many; just part of the herd. So, like animals, we are left to scramble to fill this void with worldly wants and lusts; works of the flesh.

Make no mistake about it, the influencers of our culture (media, Hollywood, TV, universities, public schools, etc.) are, by and large, godless propagandists who are determined to instill in us the notion that we are "merely animals." Therefore, women are objectified, men are just vulgar beasts, pre-born babies are a clump of cells, and the nuclear family – the bedrock of civilization – is outdated. As the Satanist Aleister Crowley said: "Do what thou wilt shall be the whole of the law." Just be animals.

After the crowd abandoned Jesus in despair, He then said to the Twelve, "Do you also want to leave?" Simon Peter answered him, "Master, to whom shall we go? You have the words of eternal life. We have come to believe and are convinced that You are the Holy One of God."

The Apostles were not buying the lie of the devil. No, we are not just animals; we are precious children of God, created in His image. Therefore, life in the Spirit is filled with the hope of a joyful and amazing journey of striving to please God in every way, especially by striving to become the best version of ourselves we can possibly be. And, just as Jesus demonstrated on the cross, we are called to a total selfless love of neighbor.

The crowd abandoned Him in despair, but the Apostles stayed with Him in hope. If we want the hope of all meaning and purpose in life as a child of God, we

> THE CROWD ABANDONED HIM IN DESPAIR, BUT THE APOSTLES STAYED WITH HIM IN HOPE.
>
> **"**

simply must get near to Him, because "the Spirit gives life."
We must combat the temptation of allowing our faith to
devolve into merely "punching the clock" by fulfilling basic
obligations. Many avoid an intimate relationship with the
Lord because, like the crowd, they believe, "This is a hard
teaching." In other words, if we "let God in" He will ask
"too much" from us. It's better to keep God at arm's length
— a manageable distance.

It's time to make it personal. It's time to get near to
Him before the Blessed Sacrament, to spend time adoring
Our Lord. This can be done by scheduling an hour at a
local adoration chapel, or you can simply come early or stay
after Mass. Be careful though, because you may just find
yourself crying out, "My Lord and my God!" ... and then
everything will change. Your life, filled with hope, will rise
to new and exciting heights!

"Those who hope in the Lord will renew their strength.
They will soar on wings like eagles; they will run and not
grow weary, they will walk and not be faint" (Isaiah 40:31).

Prayer of Reparation

My Lord and my God, we have allowed the temptation
of the devil to move our hearts to despair in Your Presence
and power. We have kept ourselves distanced from You, so
that we may be safe from Your plan for our lives. We have
been too fearful to trust in a personal relationship that may
ask too much from us. In our doubt and despair, we have
allowed the ancient foe to advance. We turn to You Lord,
in our emptiness, and beg Your forgiveness for our

despairing lack of trust. We beg for the grace to draw near to You, even as we watch, as did the Apostles, so many who abandon You. We know, Lord, if You will it, it will be done. Trusting in You, we offer our prayer to You who live and reign forever and ever. Amen.

Prayer of Exorcism

Lord God of heaven and earth, in Your power and goodness, You created all things. You set a path for us to walk on and a way to an eternal relationship. By the strength of Your arm and Word of Your mouth, cast from Your Holy Church every fearful deceit of the devil. Drive from us manifestations of the demonic that oppress us and beckon us to doubt and despair. Still the lying tongue of the devil and his forces so that we may act freely and faithfully to Your will. Send Your holy angels to cast out all influence that the demonic entities in charge of despair have planted in Your Church. Free us, our families, our parish, our diocese, and our country from all trickery and deceit perpetrated by the devil and his hellish legions. Trusting in Your goodness Lord, we know if You will it, it will be done, in unity with Your Son and the Holy Spirit, one God, forever and ever. Amen.

⏾ DAY 2 CHECKLIST ⏾

__ Prayer for Freedom from the Devil - pg. 255

__ Daily reflection and prayers

__ Litany of the day – pg. 256

__ Pray a Rosary (intention: exorcism of despair) – pg.275

__ Divine Mercy Chaplet (in reparation for: sin due to despair) – pg. 279

__ Spiritual or corporal work of mercy (see pg. 254)

__ Fast/abstain (according to level)

__ Exercise (according to level/ability)

__ Refrain from conventional media (only 1 hr. of social)

__ Examination of conscience (confession 1x this week)

Day 3
Freedom from TREASON
By FR. JAMES ALTMAN

Dear family, the very word "treason" stirs a fundamental loathing within us toward the traitor. Nobody likes a traitor, a betrayer. Indeed, as to the greatest traitor of all time, the betrayer of the Son of God, Jesus Himself said "... woe to that man by whom the Son of Man is betrayed. It would be better for that man if he had never been born" (Matthew 26:24).

The common understanding or definition of traitor is criminal disloyalty, typically to the state. It is a crime that covers some of the more extreme acts against one's nation or sovereign. Perhaps the most ancient figure that exemplifies treason is Brutus, who betrayed Julius Caesar, through whom Shakespeare had utter the famous words "et tu Brute?" – "and you, Brutus?" – even you, Brutus, my friend? Remember such similar, chilling words, spoken 2,000 years ago, "Judas, are you betraying the Son of Man with a kiss?" (Luke 22:48).

As Americans – at least before the current historical revisionism – we have known since schooldays what to think of treason. We were taught what to think through classic examples that, like every good parable, imparted to us the sense of right and wrong. On the one hand, we learned of the betrayal by Benedict Arnold, whose name has become synonymous with treason. Benjamin Franklin wrote that "Judas sold only one man, Arnold three million." On the other hand, we learned of the glorious sacrifice of Nathan Hale who, as he stood before the British gallows, uttered the renowned words "I only regret that I have but one life to lose for my country."

Who can forget the brave witness of faith of Bishop St. John Fisher who refused to apostatize himself before the malevolent King Henry VIII, whilst the rest of the cowardly episcopacy bent to the will of a mere human? Who can forget the more recent brave witnesses of the Mexican clergy-martyrs, like Blessed Miguel Pro, or the incomprehensibly brave 14-year-old boy, St. José Sánchez del Río?

It all fits together ... the secular revulsion we have toward the "Benedict Arnolds" of the world, and the revulsion we have toward the "Judases" who betrayed us in the Faith. It certainly explains the revulsion that the faithful had for the grave betrayal of the abuse scandal. It was bad enough that abuse occurred in the first place; it was immeasurably worse when certain members of the hierarchy covered it up; it was much worse than that when others who knew stood by and did nothing; and worst of all when some of the hierarchy themselves were perpetrators. The grave consequences to the faith of the faithful are well known.

But it is easy to blame those we readily identify as Judases. It is a lot easier to point the finger at other particularly evil traitors, but what about us? Let us never forget the parable Jesus taught about those who were convinced of their own righteousness. How often are we like the Pharisee who took up his position in the temple "and spoke this prayer to himself, 'O God, I thank You that I am not like the rest of humanity — greedy, dishonest, adulterous — or even like this tax collector'" (Luke 18:11).

The fact is that we all have been traitors. In fact, we all are traitors, to a greater or lesser extent maybe, but traitors, nonetheless. Every single time we betray the Sacrifice on Calvary…traitor. Every time we sin, in what we have done and in what we have failed to do…traitor. We betray the Cross of Christ every time we refuse to pick up our crosses and follow Jesus to our own personal Calvary. For today, let us look at what might be the most insidious way we betray Jesus — in what we have failed to do.

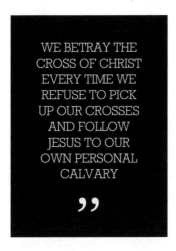

WE BETRAY THE CROSS OF CHRIST EVERY TIME WE REFUSE TO PICK UP OUR CROSSES AND FOLLOW JESUS TO OUR OWN PERSONAL CALVARY

As the great Archbishop Charles Chaput once said: "For Pope Benedict, lay people and priests don't need to publicly renounce their Catholic faith to be apostates; they simply need to be silent when their baptism demands that they speak out, to be cowards when Jesus asks them to have courage." So, what about us? What about our own treason?

Dear family, in our politically-correct-poisoned culture, we are stigmatized, chastised, and ostracized when we try to live out our Faith publicly. We are hammered by the proposition that we are being "judgmental" when we stand up for the truths of our Faith. Yet, if we speak up and speak out about the unchanged and unchangeable truth about sin, and endure the repercussions for doing so, should we not have the same attitude as Jesus to the temple guard? — "If I have spoken wrongly, testify to the wrong; but if I have spoken rightly, why do you strike me?" (John 18:23).

Let us pray this day to be free from treason – from highest treason – against Jesus our Lord, in what we do, but perhaps even more, in what we have failed to do. Too many times we have remained silent when our baptism calls us to stand up and speak out against sin in the world. Indeed, dear family, we will know we have gone spiritually blind when we can see nothing significantly wrong with something that God has called sin.

Prayer of Reparation

My Lord and my God, we have allowed the temptation of the devil to move our hearts toward treason. We have fallen into treason when we have not lived up to the call of our baptism by not acknowledging You before others. We fear the persecution in every aspect of our lives, especially those things that impact our income or our social relationships. In our weakness, we have been weak in faith, and betrayed You like Peter in the courtyard, denying You far many more times. In so many ways, we fear the ill-will of man more than we fear the loss of heaven. We turn to You Lord, in our weakness, and beg Your forgiveness for our countless betrayals. We love You, Lord, and we beg for the courage to say to others, "Yes, I know Him who is Lord of heaven and earth." We know, Lord, if You will it, it will be done. Trusting in You, we offer our prayer to You who live and reign forever and ever. Amen.

Prayer of Exorcism

Lord God of heaven and earth, in Your power and goodness, You created all things. You set a path for us to walk on and a way to an eternal relationship. By the strength of Your arm and Word of Your mouth, cast from Your Holy Church every fearful deceit of the devil. Drive from us manifestations of the demonic that oppress us and beckon us to silence and treason. Still the lying tongue of the devil and his forces so that we may act freely and faithfully to Your will. Send Your holy angels to cast out all influence that the demonic entities in charge of treason have planted in Your Church. Free us, our families, our parish, our diocese, and our country from all trickery and deceit perpetrated by the devil and his hellish legions. Trusting in Your goodness Lord, we know if You will it, it will be done, in unity with Your Son and the Holy Spirit, One God, forever and ever. Amen.

♫ DAY 3 CHECKLIST ♫

__ Prayer for Freedom from the Devil - pg. 255

__ Daily reflection and prayers

__ Litany of the day – pg. 256

__ Pray a Rosary (intention: exorcism of treason) – pg.275

__ Divine Mercy Chaplet (in reparation for: sin due to treason) – pg. 279

__ Spiritual or corporal work of mercy (see pg. 254)

__ Fast/abstain (according to level)

__ Exercise (according to level/ability)

__ Refrain from conventional media (only 1 hr. of social)

__ Examination of conscience (confession 1x this week)

Day 4
Freedom from PREDATION
By FR. WILLIAM PECKMAN

The devil is the ultimate predator. St. Peter warns his readers, "Stay sober and alert. Your opponent the devil is prowling like a roaring lion looking for someone to devour" (1 Peter 5:8). The devil is always looking for any opening in which he can pounce and destroy. He uses everything from occult practices to our concupiscence (our predilection to sin) to gain a beachhead. He will also teach us how to follow him as predators ourselves.

We live in a society that encourages predation. From the mobster who shakes down the local merchant for protection, to the sex trafficker and pornographer, to the predatory interest charged in so many loans, to the endless scams used to bilk people out of money, to the common bullying (cyber and otherwise), to those engaged in domestic violence — our society is full of predators looking for their mark, looking for their next meal. Many hide behind the cover of darkness, anonymity, or even behind the law.

Our Church has been rocked over the past half century by predation. The most obvious examples have stemmed from the scandals in which clerics preyed on their own flocks for sexual gratification, heinously even preying on the lambs of their flock. Others have preyed on their flock through financial malfeasance by defrauding their parishes or dioceses of funds. Many are also complicit in withholding from their flocks how to stave off predation. In abandoning their flocks, they are every bit as guilty as the wolves they welcomed.

Certainly, we can extend these behaviors to the most basic building block of the Church: the domestic church, or the family. In these places we can see domestic violence, molestation, and other nefarious abuses of power that have their roots in the diabolic. The demonic mimicking of the predatory behaviors of the devil must be purged from all levels of the Church.

All predatory behavior stems from selfishness: the person's needs or wants are so important that all means to satisfy them are justified. For a predator, his or her satiation is of far greater value than your happiness, security, or life. While a predator may be infatuated by their prey, they cannot love them. Their intent is to eventually destroy or discard, after they have taken all they want. What force could possibly stand up against such an insatiable beast?!

ALL PREDATORY BEHAVIOR STEMS FROM SELFISHNESS

We look to Christ the Good Shepherd for our answer! Christ does not prey on His flock. No, He places Himself between His flock and that which would destroy them. He stands in that breech, sacrificing Himself for their salvation. Jesus tells us, "I am the good shepherd; the good shepherd lays down his life for his sheep" (John 10:11). Why would He do this? Because He loves them. It is impossible to love someone and prey on them at the same time. Hence, the virtue we cultivate to conquer the desire to be a predator is the theological virtue of love. Love, divine love (or agape) is completely selfless. Instead of focusing on one's own desires and satiation, love allows you to look to the good of others, even when doing so incurs suffering or sacrifice. Love, because it is of God, chases away the devil and his minions. It helps us, as St. Paul says of himself, to be "poured out like an oblation" (2 Timothy 4:6).

Prayer of Reparation

My Lord and my God, we have allowed the temptation of the devil to move our hearts to prey on those we deem weaker or disposable. We have stilled our tongues in the face of such evil. We have been too fearful to stand out in our culture, allowing selfish desires to suffocate Your love that is to dwell within us. In our fear, we have allowed the ancient foe to advance. We turn to You Lord, in our sorrow and guilt, and beg Your forgiveness for our selfishness and silence. We beg for the grace of Your goodness to teach us to shepherd rightly those You place in our care, and the courage to stand in the breech between them and the demonic. Help us to love as You love. We know, Lord, if You will it, it will be done. Trusting in You, we offer our prayer to You who live and reign forever and ever. Amen.

Prayer of Exorcism

Lord God of heaven and earth, in Your power and goodness, You created all things. You set a path for us to walk on and a way to an eternal relationship. By the strength of Your arm and Word of Your mouth, cast from Your Holy Church every fearful deceit of the devil. Drive from us manifestations of the demonic that oppress us and beckon us to selfishness and predation. Still the lying tongue of the devil and his forces so that we may act freely and faithfully to Your will. Send Your holy angels to cast out all influence that the demonic entities in charge of predation have planted in Your Church. Free us, our families, our parish, our diocese, and our country from all trickery and deceit perpetrated by the devil and his hellish legions. Trusting in Your goodness Lord, we know if You will it, it will be done, in unity with Your Son and the Holy Spirit, one God, forever and ever. Amen.

🔔 DAY 4 CHECKLIST 🔔

___ Prayer for Freedom from the Devil - pg. 255

___ Daily reflection and prayers

___ Litany of the day – pg. 256

___ Pray a Rosary (intention: exorcism of predation) – pg.275

___ Divine Mercy Chaplet (in reparation for: sin due to predation) – pg. 279

___ Spiritual or corporal work of mercy (see pg. 254)

___ Fast/abstain (according to level)

___ Exercise (according to level/ability)

___ Refrain from conventional media (only 1 hr. of social)

___ Examination of conscience (confession 1x this week)

Day 5
Freedom from COWARDICE
By FR. RICHARD HEILMAN

Recently, Facebook suspended my account for 24 hours for sharing a video of a respected doctor who has had success with a treatment for COVID-19. The video that supposedly does not follow Facebook's community standards had 1.5 million views in one week, and at the time of this writing has not been banned on YouTube.

What's going on here? Obviously, this is about the ongoing threat of my willingness to speak the truth openly. Such behavior is not allowed by the mob who is clearly in power now. This action by Facebook is an example of the classic chilling effect meant to place fear in anyone who does not stay within the lines of the mob's agenda. "Chilling effect" is a term in law and communication that describes a situation where speech or conduct is suppressed by fear of penalization at the interests of an individual or group.

The problem right now is that this chilling effect is proving to be remarkably effective. Most people are cowering in fear. Even religious leaders are kowtowing to the mob. Why? Because speaking the truth openly is considered "divisive." In other words, because those who oppose the Holy Spirit aggressively express their offense of divine revelation (Sacred Scripture and Sacred Tradition), we must remain silent on these teachings. For the sake of unity, we are expected to silently sit by and allow the normalization of killing babies, the demise of the nuclear family, sodomy, gender dysphoria (grown men sharing a bathroom with little girls), Marxism, etc.

These growing calls for silence, amid the mounting aggression of the mob, have turned an incrementalism of evil into a bum-rush of everything that betrays the will of God.

Archbishop Fulton Sheen wrote, "The refusal to take sides on great moral issues is itself a decision. It is a silent acquiescence to evil. The tragedy of our time is that those who still believe in honesty lack fire and conviction, while those who believe in dishonesty are full of passionate conviction."

> THE TRAGEDY OF OUR TIME IS THAT THOSE WHO STILL BELIEVE IN HONESTY LACK FIRE AND CONVICTION, WHILE THOSE WHO BELIEVE IN DISHONESTY ARE FULL OF PASSIONATE CONVICTION
>
> "

Jesus did not prescribe this silent acquiescence to evil as a way to avoid division. We are not to kowtow to any chilling effect from the mob. Instead, we must be willing to boldly speak the truth with love, despite the backlash that is sure to come. We were told, "Brother will hand over brother to death, and the father his child; children will rise up against parents and have them put to death. You will be hated by all because of my name, but whoever endures to the end will be saved" (Matthew 10:21-22).

There it is — "but whoever endures to the end will be saved." Therefore, I must ask myself, "What if I get hit by a car today and must stand before the judgment throne of God?" Will I be eternally condemned for speaking truth that might have been divisive or offended people? Or will I be saved because I stood with Christ and His truth, endured in fortitude, and was unafraid to thwart the advancement of evil in our times, regardless of what the consequences were?

What will YOU choose…courage or cowardice?

Prayer of Reparation

My Lord and my God, we have allowed the temptation of the devil to move our hearts toward cowardice. We have allowed the aggression of evil to make us recoil in fear. We have been too cowardly to openly stand with You and Your truth. In our fear and silence, we have allowed the ancient foe to advance. We turn to You Lord, in our shame, and beg Your forgiveness for our cowardly silence. We beg for the grace of Your strength and power to grant us the resolve to turn back the falsehoods of the enemy by freely and openly speaking Your truth with love to a waiting world. We know Lord, if You will it, it will be done. Trusting in You, we offer our prayer to You who live and reign forever and ever. Amen.

Prayer of Exorcism

Lord God of heaven and earth, in Your power and goodness, You created all things. You set a path for us to walk on and a way to an eternal relationship. By the strength of Your arm and Word of Your mouth, cast from Your Holy Church every fearful deceit of the devil. Drive from us manifestations of the demonic that oppress us and beckon us to timidity and cowardice. Still the lying tongue of the devil and his forces so that we may act freely and faithfully to Your will. Send Your holy angels to cast out all influence that the demonic entities in charge of cowardice have planted in Your Church. Free us, our families, our parish, our diocese, and our country from all trickery and deceit perpetrated by the devil and his hellish legions. Trusting in Your goodness Lord, we know if You will it, it will be done, in unity with Your Son and the Holy Spirit, one God, forever and ever. Amen.

DAY 5 CHECKLIST

__ Prayer for Freedom from the Devil - pg. 255

__ Daily reflection and prayers

__ Litany of the day – pg. 256

__ Pray a Rosary (intention: exorcism of cowardice) – pg.275

__ Divine Mercy Chaplet (in reparation for: sin due to cowardice) – pg. 279

__ Spiritual or corporal work of mercy (see pg. 254)

__ Fast/abstain (according to level)

__ Exercise (according to level/ability)

__ Refrain from conventional media (only 1 hr. of social)

__ Examination of conscience (confession 1x this week)

Day 6
Freedom from VENGEANCE
By FR. JAMES ALTMAN

Dear family, vengeance sounds a whole lot like revenge to me, both of which we know in our hearts are not good things. One site tried to explain the difference: "the difference between revenge and vengeance is that revenge is any form of personal retaliatory action against an individual, institution, or group for some perceived harm or injustice while vengeance is revenge taken for an insult, injury, or other wrong." Well, that was no help! They still sound like the same thing. Sure enough, another site called the words synonyms.

In any event, this we know: "Vengeance is Mine, saith the Lord" (Deuteronomy 32:35). The truth in Deuteronomy is found in the words of St. Paul, "Beloved, do not look for revenge but leave room for the wrath; for it is written, 'Vengeance is mine, I will repay,' says the Lord" (Romans 12:19). When the Word became Flesh and dwelt among us, He confirmed it all, teaching: "You have heard that it was said, 'An eye for an eye and a tooth for a tooth.' But I say to you, offer no resistance to one who is evil. When someone strikes you on (your) right cheek, turn the other one to him as well" (Matthew 5:38-39).

What does "offer no resistance to one who is evil" mean exactly? In our day and age, this is an important question that is, unfortunately, too often answered with a glib and meaningless recitation of "turn the other cheek."

This response though is a disconnected scriptural verse, taken out of context, out of culture, and out of text written about 2,000 years ago in a language that few people understand.

Let us begin with what Matthew 5:38-39 really means. The biblical notes to those two verses state: "The Old Testament commandment was meant to moderate vengeance; the punishment should not exceed the injury done. Jesus forbids even this proportionate retaliation." Right away then, we see this only pertains to the concept of retaliation. It did not mean then, and it does not mean now, that we simply lay down and play "doormat" for any evil doer.

This "I'm not a doormat" principle may be explained best by considering self-defense. We are entitled to protect our own lives and the lives of others. This right is not negated by Jesus' teachings, and in fact, it stands in contrast to the scriptural admonition against retaliation. The warning against retaliation may be understood by pondering one of its consequences: escalation. For example, one bad actor "A" incites retaliation from "B", which incites retaliation from "A", which incites more retaliation from "B", etc. This vengeance cycle can escalate to the point where others end up getting caught in the crossfire. In the real world this results in bodies in the streets of our cities, and innocent victims (too often little children) reaping the repercussions.

In a larger sense, who can deny that the current culture of violence, rioting, looting, and burning is nothing other than vengeance and retaliation? The anarchists set themselves up against Christian truth, truth found in the words of the great prophet Jeremiah: "To whom shall I speak? Whom shall I warn and be heard? ... See, the word of the LORD has become for them an object of scorn, for which they have no taste" (Jeremiah 6:10). It explains why the Seattle mayor's absurd response to CHOP (the Capitol Hill Organized Protest) seems to prevail everywhere – remember she called it "the summer of love." We saw the "love" in the murders and violent crimes. Her perverse twisting of truth also is found in the words of Jeremiah: "They have treated lightly the injury to my people: 'Peace, peace!' they say, though there is no peace" (Jeremiah 6:14).

In a more personal sense, all that we are seeing is nothing other than a reflection of people's hearts devoid of the tempering grace of Divine Love. Divine Love did not rain down lightning bolts upon the Roman centurions who drove the nails into His sacred body. Rather, Jesus sought to show Divine Love when He asked our Father to forgive them, for they knew not what they did (cf. Luke 23:34).

Let us realize, though, that Jesus did not paint with a broad brush of forgiveness to include those who knew what they were doing, or those who should have known. That is why Jesus said the members of the Sanhedrin who condemned Him would not enter the Kingdom of Heaven (cf. Matthew 5:20). That is why God's justice will have its day when the lack of love drives so many to act in a vengeful way.

Again, the opposite of vengeance is love. But love is not demonstrated by playing "doormat." In the face of evil, genuine love is known as "tough love."

TRUE LOVE SPEAKS UP AND SPEAKS OUT WITH COURAGE, IN THE FACE OF GRAVE ERROR THAT THREATENS REAL PEACE

True love speaks up and speaks out with courage, in the face of grave error that threatens real peace. True love is enshrined in the spiritual works of mercy that teach us to instruct the ignorant and admonish the sinner. Instruction and admonishment are correction, they are not the same as vengeance or retaliation.

In these dark times, let us not fall into the trap of a false mercy, some twisted interpretation of "turning the other cheek." Rather let us be a Light of Christ and an example of genuine love that instructs the ignorant and admonishes the sinner. Amidst all the vengeance we see in the streets, and in the personal hurts in our own lives, we will have plenty of opportunity to do that. So, any time we find ourselves struggling with thoughts of vengeance instead of mercy, let us make haste to spend more time before the Blessed Sacrament, meditating upon the Holy Cross, where the Light of Christ enlightens the darkest thoughts of our own souls.

Prayer of Reparation

My Lord and my God, we have allowed the temptation of the devil to move our hearts toward vengeance. We have allowed works of evil to foment within us a heart of retaliation. Worse, through our own sins of omission, we have not come to a fuller understanding of Your truth about the difference between a heart dark with the spirit of vengeance, that expresses itself in acts of evil against others, and the heart enlightened by love and mercy, that expresses itself in instruction and admonishment of others. By allowing our hearts to move toward darkness and not toward the Light, we have allowed the ancient foe to advance in our streets and in ourselves. We turn to You Lord, in our shame, and beg Your forgiveness for any heart of dark vengeance and any failure to be the light of love. We beg for the grace of Your strength and power to grant us the resolve to turn back the falsehoods of the enemy by freely and openly speaking Your truth with love to a waiting world. We know, Lord, if You will it, it will be done. Trusting in You, we offer our prayer to You, who live and reign forever and ever. Amen.

Prayer of Exorcism

Lord God of heaven and earth, in Your power and goodness, You created all things. You set a path for us to walk on and a way to an eternal relationship. By the strength of Your arm and Word of Your mouth, cast from Your Holy Church every fearful deceit of the devil. Drive from us manifestations of the demonic that oppress us and beckon us to revenge and retaliation. Still the lying tongue of the devil and his forces so that we may act freely and faithfully in imitation of You. Send Your holy angels to cast out all influence that the demonic entities in charge of vengeance have planted in Your Church. Free us, our families, our parish, our diocese, and our country from all trickery and deceit perpetrated by the devil and his hellish legions. Trusting in Your goodness Lord, we know if You will it, it will be done, in unity with Your Son and the Holy Spirit, one God forever and ever. Amen.

🔔 DAY 6 CHECKLIST 🔔

__ Prayer for Freedom from the Devil - pg. 255

__ Daily reflection and prayers

__ Litany of the day – pg. 256

__ Pray a Rosary (intention: exorcism of vengeance) – pg.275

__ Divine Mercy Chaplet (in reparation for: sin due to vengeance) – pg. 279

__ Spiritual or corporal work of mercy (see pg. 254)

__ Fast/abstain (according to level)

__ Exercise (according to level/ability)

__ Refrain from conventional media (only 1 hr. of social)

__ Examination of conscience (confession 1x this week)

Day 7
Freedom from ENVY
By FR. WILLIAM PECKMAN

It is the green-eyed monster that mocks what it feeds upon. In *Othello*, Iago warns Othello of the green-eyed monster that we know as jealousy or envy. How appropriate that the deadly sin of envy should be given a monstrous or demonic personage! Envy is the resentment one feels for the success or good of another. It is not necessarily directed only at enemies but also at one's family and friends, which leads to the German term *schadenfreude* (leave it to our German ancestors to have an extensive vocabulary for pain).

In the Gospel of Mark, 9:38-40, the apostles come across a man who is exorcising demons in Jesus' name and they try to stop him. Jesus responds by telling them to let the man be, as anyone who is with Him cannot be against Him. We see time and again the envy of the religious leaders who persecute Jesus, seeking ways to trap Him in the process of showing mercy. Envy, as Shakespeare noted, mocks what it feeds on because it is incapable of rejoicing in the good of another.

Envy is pervasive in our society. We are taught to resent the success of others as if somehow it threatens our identity or morale. We are taught to resent the belongings of others as if they somehow came from our portion of the pie. We are taught to find excuses in our perpetual victimhood that can be laid at the feet of those who succeed. Some political movements, such as Marxism, rely on envy to stir resentment that destroys the social order. Envy leads us to demonize the successful, to seek their downfall, to denigrate their talents, and to destroy their reputations. It is much easier to tear someone down than it is to convert oneself to something greater.

Such a mentality can find itself in our churches. I worked in the business world for several years prior to going into the seminary; I have seen and climbed the corporate ladder. On those rungs, I did not see nearly the amount of professional

IT IS MUCH EASIER TO TEAR SOMEONE DOWN THAN IT IS TO CONVERT ONESELF TO SOMETHING GREATER

jealousy that I have seen among those who work in the Church. Envy and ambition are constant companions. I have seen volunteers tear down and wish failure upon other volunteers because they were envious of their success. I have seen this in priests and have been guilty myself, from time to time, during my over 23 years of priestly ministry. Envy is as destructive within the Body of Christ as it is outside of it.

How do we combat such a demonic presence? Let us go back to the response of Christ in Mark 9: "No man who performs a miracle using my name can at the same time speak ill of me. Anyone who is not against us is with us." The apostles should have rejoiced that the man in question was exorcising in Jesus' name. They should have seen his success as Christ's success. Hence, part of defeating the demonic influence is learning to share in the joy of those who have succeeded justly and to pray for the redemption of those who have succeeded under nefarious means. Either leads us closer to our Christian call. Cultivate joy at the good. Cultivate mercy through prayer for the bad.

Another way to combat envy is thanksgiving. Gratitude for what God has done, and continues to do, will do more to alleviate the grasp of the green-eyed monster than anything else. It is easy to be envious when one has a dearth of thanksgiving. When one is truly thankful, one has less time and inclination to be envious of what others have or who others are. This thankfulness leads to a generosity and a correct stewardship of what God has given us. Nothing so starves and chases away the green-eyed monster of envy quite the way a heart full of thankfulness does.

Finally, one must cultivate the virtue of humility. Humility seeks the truth about oneself, both good and bad, and restrains us from getting caught up in the tentacles of envy. A good example of this can be found in St. Paul's first letter to the Corinthians. St. Paul is tempted to resent Peter and Apollos in their preaching in Corinth. Although none of these three men saw themselves as anything other than being of the team, the people of Corinth had allowed division based on who said what. In St. Paul's response, a plea for unity in Christ, he does not defend himself as greater than Peter or Apollos, rather he humbles himself. He acknowledges that God uses each as He deems fit.

Humility, because it is bound in truth, enables us to rejoice in the good of our brothers, to be thankful for what God does for us, and to have an attitude of mercy.

Prayer of Reparation

My Lord and my God, we have allowed the temptation of the devil to move our hearts to resent the blessings You bestow on others and to be blinded to the blessings You have given to us. We have allowed the thanksgiving we should have for You to become resentment and envy. We have been too fearful to stand out in our culture, allowing selfish desires to suffocate Your love that is to dwell within us. In our fear, we have allowed the ancient foe to advance. We turn to You Lord, in our sorrow and guilt, and beg Your forgiveness for our thanklessness and resentment. We beg for the grace of Your goodness so we can rejoice in Your goodness to others and be truly thankful for the many gifts You bestow on us. Help us to love as You love. We know, Lord, if You will it, it will be done. Trusting in You, we offer our prayer to You who live and reign forever and ever. Amen.

Prayer of Exorcism

Lord God of heaven and earth, in Your power and goodness, You created all things. You set a path for us to walk on and a way to an eternal relationship. By the strength of Your arm and Word of Your mouth, cast from Your Holy Church every fearful deceit of the devil. Drive from us manifestations of the demonic that oppress us and beckon us to resentment, envy, and thanklessness. Still the lying tongue of the devil and his forces so that we may act freely and faithfully in imitation of You. Send Your holy angels to cast out all influence that the demonic entities in charge of envy have planted in Your Church. Free us, our families, our parish, our diocese, and our country from all trickery and deceit perpetrated by the devil and his hellish legions. Trusting in Your goodness Lord, we know if You will it, it will be done, in unity with Your Son and the Holy Spirit, one God forever and ever. Amen.

🔔 DAY 7 CHECKLIST 🔔

__ Prayer for Freedom from the Devil - pg. 255

__ Daily reflection and prayers

__ Litany of the day – pg. 256

__ Pray a Rosary (intention: exorcism of envy) – pg.275

__ Divine Mercy Chaplet (in reparation for: sin due to envy) – pg. 279

__ Spiritual or corporal work of mercy (see pg. 254)

__ Fast/abstain (according to level)

__ Exercise (according to level/ability)

__ Refrain from conventional media (only 1 hr. of social)

__ Examination of conscience (confession 1x this week)

Day 8
Freedom from ELITISM
By FR. RICHARD HEILMAN

In an interview with Carl E. Olson, Dr. Angelo Codevilla, author of the book, *The Ruling Class*, said:

"The ruling class are society's 'ins.' This class comprises persons in government, those who depend for their livelihoods on government, and whose socio-economic prospects and hopes are founded on government. Thus, it includes most people in the educational establishment, the media, and large corporations. Its leading elements and its major voting constituencies are the Democratic party. But it transcends political parties because any number of Republicans aspire to its privileges and share its priorities.

"Above all, the ruling class defines itself by a set of attitudes, foremost of which is contempt for those outside itself. This contempt stems from the rather uniform education that the ruling class's members absorbed from universities and which they developed by living in their subculture. Believing themselves intelligent apostles of scientific truth, they regard others as dumb and in the grip of religious obscurantism. Religion is the greatest of the divides between the ruling class and those it deems its inferiors. Whereas they believe themselves morally good and psychologically sound, they regard others as suffering from psychological dysfunctions and phobias – effectively as bad people. The ruling class does not believe that those outside itself have the right or capacity to conduct their own lives."

The rest of us, often described as the "country class" or, as the 2016 Democratic presidential candidate called us, "deplorables," comprise most of our country. Nevertheless, the secular religion of the ruling class has captured virtually all the sources of influence: the media, Hollywood, TV, universities, public schools, etc. At the same time, unfortunately, many religious leaders seem to be tripping over themselves with shameless attempts to ingratiate themselves with this secular religion's high priests.

In today's culture, this elitism has seemed to take control, as speech or conduct contrary to the agenda of the elites is suppressed with threats: threats against reputation, employment, property, and even one's physical safety. Let's call it what it is: They are bullies. Operating from moral relativism, which proclaims the end always justifies the means, everything – EVERYTHING! – is on the table for accomplishing the elites' goal of gaining complete power and control.

Elitism is the temptation of every human being, and we have all recognized it as early as our childhood days when the so-called "cool kids" on the playground would exert their superiority, often by ridiculing those they deemed as "beneath" them. The temptation is to compromise, surrender, or even join ranks with these elites of our day. No! Jesus calls us to be the "mighty influencers" of our culture, to be "disrupters." We are called not to promote the selfish "establishment" and their power-hungry and godless agenda, but to promote the virtues, morals, values, and ethics of God's kingdom.

The influence of the elites is strong, and in many ways, we have grown weak. More than any other time, WE NEED EACH OTHER! We need to become UNIFIED! We need to do all we can to spend as much time as possible with others who are striving to GET STRONG in the virtues of God's Kingdom. Proverbs 27:17 says, "Iron sharpens iron, so one man sharpens another."

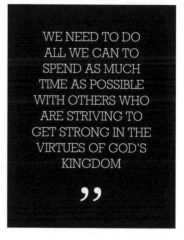

WE NEED TO DO ALL WE CAN TO SPEND AS MUCH TIME AS POSSIBLE WITH OTHERS WHO ARE STRIVING TO GET STRONG IN THE VIRTUES OF GOD'S KINGDOM

Parishes were always meant to be these epicenters of unity and strength. Parishes simply must work to be the best possible "spiritual gymnasiums" they can be, where those who attend are encouraged, challenged, and instructed in all the ways to become "strong in the Lord and in His mighty power" (Ephesians 6:10). Parishes must be places where we find fellow Catholics who "spur one another on toward love and good deeds" (Hebrews 10:24).

I'm sure you are, like me, long past tired of the ruling class's mob claiming the moral high ground with their demonically influenced secular religion. It's high time for all of us to become a force to be reckoned with, UNITED in our resolve to GET STRONG in God's mighty power!

Prayer of Reparation

My Lord and my God, we have allowed the temptation of the devil to move our hearts toward elitism. We have allowed works of evil to foment within us a heart needing approval. We have been divided and weak in our lack of resolve to seek the unity and spiritual strength to resist the elites of our culture today. In our fear and silent self-protection, we have allowed the ancient foe to advance. We turn to You Lord, in our shame, and beg Your forgiveness for our lack of resolve. We beg for the grace of Your strength and power to grant us the resolve to turn back the falsehoods of the enemy by freely and openly speaking Your truth with love to a waiting world. We know, Lord, if You will it, it will be done. Trusting in You, we offer our prayer to You who live and reign forever and ever. Amen.

Prayer of Exorcism

Lord God of heaven and earth, in Your power and goodness, You created all things. You set a path for us to walk on and a way to an eternal relationship. By the strength of Your arm and Word of Your mouth, cast from Your Holy Church every fearful deceit of the devil. Drive from us manifestations of the demonic that oppress us and beckon us to elitism and division. Still the lying tongue of the devil and his forces so that we may act freely and faithfully in imitation of You. Send Your holy angels to cast out all influence that the demonic entities in charge of elitism have planted in Your Church. Free us, our families, our parish, our diocese, and our country from all trickery and deceit perpetrated by the devil and his hellish legions. Trusting in Your goodness Lord, we know if You will it, it will be done, in unity with Your Son and the Holy Spirit, one God forever and ever. Amen.

☖ DAY 8 CHECKLIST ☖

__ Prayer for Freedom from the Devil - pg. 255

__ Daily reflection and prayers

__ Litany of the day – pg. 256

__ Pray a Rosary (intention: exorcism of elitism) – pg.275

__ Divine Mercy Chaplet (in reparation for: sin due to elitism) – pg. 279

__ Spiritual or corporal work of mercy (see pg. 254)

__ Fast/abstain (according to level)

__ Exercise (according to level/ability)

__ Refrain from conventional media (only 1 hr. of social)

__ Examination of conscience (confession 1x this week)

Day 9

Freedom from ABUSE OF SEXUALITY OUTSIDE OF THE MARITAL STATE

By FR. JAMES ALTMAN

Dear family, it is time to speak truth, and speak it boldly, on the issue of the abuse of sexuality outside of the marital state, which can best be understood by the phrase "interim period." There is a dichotomy in this world: God and Lucifer. God has His plan, and it is Good. Lucifer has his plan, which is the opposite of God's, and it is evil. Once we confess and admit what God's intention actually is, we then can identify, recognize, and avoid Lucifer's evil plan while striving to follow God's good one. Lucifer's scheme is evil in all its insidious and diabolical facets, most particularly in artificial contraception, cohabitation, abortion, and same-sex unions.

God's good plan is simple, straightforward, and easy to understand: "God created mankind in His image; in the image of God He created them; male and female He created them. God blessed them and God said to them: 'Be fertile and multiply; fill the earth and subdue it'" (Genesis 1:27-28). "The LORD God said: 'It is not good for the man to be alone. I will make a helper suited to him' ... The LORD God then built the rib that He had taken from the man into a woman. ... That is why a man leaves his father and mother and clings to his wife, and the two of them become one body" (Genesis 2:18, 22, 24).

That is God's plan, that is the truth, and anything contrary to the truth is false. That is known as the PNC, the Principle of Non-Contradiction. Therefore, anything contrary to one man, one woman, open to children, for life is false. Period. End of debate. So how did we ever get to the point where any Christian dares to suggest, much less insist, that artificial contraception, co-habitation outside the sacramental bond of matrimony, termination of a baby's life in the womb, and same-sex unions are A-OK with God? With what twisted and diabolical poison have we been fed? Here is how all this happened: greed and selfishness.

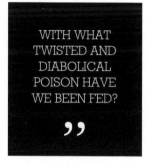

WITH WHAT TWISTED AND DIABOLICAL POISON HAVE WE BEEN FED?

99

In God's creation, and throughout millennia, boys and girls reached puberty roughly at 12-14 years of age. Having a very developed brain by the age of roughly 12, they were mature enough to be able to cope with the onset of hormonal challenges while they were in the safety and security of their family homes. Then, when fully mature, the young man would leave the family home for the purpose of getting married and thereafter cling to his wife. There was no interim period between leaving the family home and marriage. Not in God's plan, which is the only plan that matters.

Then diabolical greed came into the picture. The food supply was tainted by steroids and growth hormones, all for the purpose of profiteering. This tainted food affected the physiological development of children even before birth, when the mother's own food was tainted. This taint has affected physiological development such that our children's bodies are maturing before their brains. In fact, this introduction into the children's bodies even affects the development of the brain, not unlike the introduction of alcohol at a certain point of pre-birth development causes the irreversible damage of fetal-alcohol syndrome. In short, earlier onset of puberty comes before God intended and at a time the child's brain and the child are not mature enough to handle it.

Then, instead of leaving the family home for the purpose of marriage, the young adult leaves the home to go to college, and "God forbid" someone gets married before graduating from college. There is an issue of economic greed at play. In fact, even after college, the young adult is discouraged from entering sacramental matrimony because, well, "I have to get my career started." Again, it is an issue of economic greed. And then, "God forbid we have kids right out of the starting block. We need time to get settled." Again, there is an issue of economic greed at play.

In society today, it is the norm to delay marriage for materialistic and relativistic reasons. Over time, the aforementioned factors have widened the gap between the average onset of physical maturity and the typical age of entrance into a sacramental marriage, making it harder for people to remain chaste.

Despite the change in society's norms, God's good plan still expects us to remain pure and chaste before sacred matrimony. Is it any wonder that so many fail so badly when faced with the challenge of living up to God's plan, and why we justify divergence from God's plan with relativistic Luciferian terms?

The results, of course, are obvious to anyone with courage enough to admit it. The results are exactly as Pope St. Paul VI said they would be when he wrote *Humanae Vitae*. The results are exactly as our Blessed Mother warned us about at Fatima — that the final battle would be an attack on God's plan for family. That is the ultimate "Russian error" of which she spoke. Hence, we have rampant contraception, cohabitation, baby-murdering, and homosexuality. (Ironically, all of these were inherent in the Albigensian heresy.)

There is not space in this reflection to discuss the totality of reasons why there is such horrific abuse of sexuality outside of the marital state. There is not space to describe the foundations and causes of the fall into contraception, the utter horror of baby murdering in the womb, the flagrant disregard of our bodies as the temples of the Holy Spirit through cohabitation, as well as the psychological reasons for the development of same-sex attraction. Fortunately, we do not have to go into great depth to find the truth about any of it. It all is founded in the simple and definitive principle that we have chosen to diverge from God's plan, and among the greatest underlying causes is greed.

Prayer of Reparation

My Lord and my God, we have allowed the temptation of the devil to move our hearts toward impurity and grave errors in sexuality. We have allowed works of evil to foment within us a heart of unchastity and immorality. Worse, through our own stubborn, prideful justification for our sins of impurity, we have not come to a fuller understanding of Your truth about the difference between God's creation and plan for family and the destruction wrought by Lucifer's plan, which is any-and-all-things-contrary to God's plan. By allowing our hearts to move toward the darkness of impurity and not toward the pure light of chastity, we have allowed the ancient foe to advance in ourselves, revealed in the destruction of family. We turn to You Lord, in our shame, and beg Your forgiveness for any heart of impurity and any failure to strive for a heart of chastity. We beg for the grace of Your strength and power to grant us the resolve to turn back the falsehoods of the enemy by freely and openly speaking Your truth with love to a waiting world. We know, Lord, if You will it, it will be done. Trusting in You, we offer our prayer to You who live and reign forever and ever. Amen.

Prayer of Exorcism

Lord God of heaven and earth, in Your power and goodness, You created all things. You set a path for us to walk on and a way to an eternal relationship. By the strength of Your arm and Word of Your mouth, cast from Your Holy Church every fearful deceit of the devil. Drive

from us manifestations of the demonic that oppress us and beckon us to unchastity and immorality. Still the lying tongue of the devil and his forces so that we may act freely and faithfully in imitation of You. Send Your holy angels to cast out all influence that the demonic entities in charge of immorality have planted in Your Church. Free us, our families, our parish, our diocese, and our country from all trickery and deceit perpetrated by the devil and his hellish legions. Trusting in Your goodness Lord, we know if You will it, it will be done, in unity with Your Son and the Holy Spirit, one God forever and ever. Amen.

🔔 DAY 9 CHECKLIST 🔔

__ Prayer for Freedom from the Devil - pg. 255
__ Daily reflection and prayers
__ Litany of the day – pg. 256
__ Pray a Rosary (intention: exorcism of abuse of sexuality outside the marriage state) – pg.275
__ Divine Mercy Chaplet (in reparation for: sin due to abuse of sexuality outside the marriage state) – pg. 279
__ Spiritual or corporal work of mercy (see pg. 254)
__ Fast/abstain (according to level)
__ Exercise (according to level/ability)
__ Refrain from conventional media (only 1 hr. of social)
__ Examination of conscience (confession 1x this week)

Day 10
Freedom from BELLIGERENCE
By FR. WILLIAM PECKMAN

In the Shakespeare play *Julius Caesar*, there is a scene in which Marc Anthony is alone with the body of the freshly assassinated Julius Caesar. He seeks vengeance on the assassins knowing it will send Rome into a killing frenzy. From this scene we hear the words, "Cry 'havoc' and let slip the dogs of war!" (*Julius Caesar* Act III, Scene I). This refrain plays all too quickly in our society as we fall into hellish nightmares of belligerence and anarchy.

The word belligerence comes from the Latin words *bellum* (war) and *genere* (to bear or carry) and means a person engaged in war. In common usage, a belligerent person is one who looks for and pursues reasons to stir trouble and engage in violent revenge. The father of belligerence is none other than he who fomented the first ever revolution against God: the devil.

We live in a horribly belligerent society right now. So many refer to being "triggered," or easily and frequently offended in such a way that justifies both the tenacity and disproportionate nature of their vengeance. The belligerent see themselves as victims of injustice whose suffering, real or imagined, is sufficient grounds for any destruction and mayhem they may engage in to address the injustice. They wreak havoc in the lives of all who around them. It is as if they look for (even long for) reasons to be angry so that they may act out without regards for consequences.

That belligerence finds itself in our churches as well. There are so many ways in which we find ourselves willfully polarized by everything from music to ritual to leadership. Some of the most hateful things I have seen posted on social media over the years have been Catholics showing a truly hateful belligerence to their fellow Catholics. I have often noted how Satan cackles at our circular firing squads. As in the secular world, belligerence is all about the accrual of power.

There are times we will not be able to avoid the belligerence of others in our defense and propagation of the truth. Jesus Himself refers multiple times to parent being set against child and child against parent as some accept and follow Christ. How do we answer belligerence? How do we stave off the desire to become belligerent against all but Satan and his minions?

The answer, I believe, can be found in Matthew 11:28-30: "Come to me, all you that labor and are burdened, and I will refresh you. Take up My yoke upon you and learn of me because I am meek, and humble of heart: and you shall find rest to your souls. For My yoke is sweet and My burden light." In this we see that our lives will come with burdens, pains, injustices, and sorrows. We will have that temptation to return belligerence for belligerence. Certainly, Christ carried this reality right up the cross.

The answer lies in our willingness and ability to show meekness. Meekness has a bad reputation as the quality of being mousy, timid, or weak.

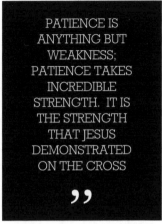

PATIENCE IS ANYTHING BUT WEAKNESS; PATIENCE TAKES INCREDIBLE STRENGTH. IT IS THE STRENGTH THAT JESUS DEMONSTRATED ON THE CROSS

Meekness is patience, a virtue that St Paul in Galatians 5:22 reminds us is a fruit of the Holy Spirit. Patience is anything but weakness; patience takes incredible strength. It is the strength that Jesus demonstrated on the cross. He shows His strength in patience and endurance. The time for judgment will come. It will be just.

Our ability to show meekness in the face of harm neither condones the harm done to us nor allows another to treat us as a doormat. It shows the strength of character that reduces the mocking and ridicule, thus providing a far stronger witness to all. Our war footing should be directed to the devil and his forces; with them we should show nothing but scorn and forcefulness. The devil and his demons have no hope of conversion. They are eternally damned. As for our fellow human beings, if they are on this side of the moment of death, the possibility, however slim, exists for possible conversion. The Church exists for the salvation of souls. Driving belligerence from our hearts and souls helps us endure the yoke of Christ: the ability to selflessly love and show unswerving obedience to the will of the Father in all things. Our only cry to release "havoc and the dogs of war" should be against the devil and his minions.

Prayer of Reparation

My Lord and my God, we have allowed the temptation of the devil to move our hearts to belligerence and wrath. We have allowed the desire to gain power to be reason to crush others. We have been so fearful of being considered weak by the world that we have embraced impatience and violence as virtuous. In our fear, we have allowed the ancient foe to advance. We turn to You Lord, in our sorrow and guilt, and beg Your forgiveness for our belligerence and rebellion against Your command to love our enemies. We beg for the grace of Your goodness to build up within us the strength and endurance You exhibited on the Cross. We know, Lord, if You will it, it will be done. Trusting in You, we offer our prayer to You who live and reign forever. Amen.

Prayer of Exorcism

Lord God of heaven and earth, in Your power and goodness, You created all things. You set a path for us to walk on and a way to an eternal relationship. By the strength of Your arm and Word of Your mouth, cast from Your Holy Church every fearful deceit of the devil. Drive from us manifestations of the demonic that oppress us and beckon us to belligerence and rebellion. Still the lying tongue of the devil and his forces so that we may act freely and faithfully to Your will. Send Your holy angels to cast out all influence that the demonic entities in charge of belligerence have planted in Your Church. Free us, our families, our parish, our diocese, and our country from all trickery and deceit perpetrated by the devil and his hellish legions. Trusting in Your goodness Lord, we know if You will it, it will be done, in unity with Your Son and the Holy Spirit, one God forever and ever. Amen.

🔔 DAY 10 CHECKLIST 🔔

__ Prayer for Freedom from the Devil - pg. 255

__ Daily reflection and prayers

__ Litany of the day – pg. 256

__ Pray a Rosary (intention: exorcism of belligerence) – pg.275

__ Divine Mercy Chaplet (in reparation for: sin due to belligerence) – pg. 279

__ Spiritual or corporal work of mercy (see pg. 254)

__ Fast/abstain (according to level)

__ Exercise (according to level/ability)

__ Refrain from conventional media (only 1 hr. of social)

__ Examination of conscience (confession 1x this week)

Day 11
Freedom from LUST
By FR. RICHARD HEILMAN

One of the most effective weapons of the devil today is lust. Our Lady of Fatima revealed, "more souls go to Hell because of sins of the flesh than for any other reason." It's more than interesting to note that Margaret Sanger opened the first birth control clinic in 1916, just as the angel first appeared to the children in Fatima. The "roaring twenties" would then burst onto the scene shortly after Our Lady's dire warning, which seemed to be "a leak in the dike" of a more debased view of sexuality.

But the dam would burst wide open with our modern-day sexual revolution. It was in the 1965 case of Griswold v. Connecticut that the Supreme Court would strike down state laws prohibiting contraception. This would be quickly followed in 1973 by the infamous Supreme Court case of Roe v. Wade, which legalized the killing of pre-born children in all states.

Once the "consequence of conception" seemed to be removed, or the legal right to kill pre-born babies was made available, the sexual revolution flooded into our culture. Now, we are seeing the "normalization" (socially acceptable) of sex-for-pleasure outside the bond of holy matrimony and the explosion of easy access pornography.

Fr. Robert Fromageot, F.S.S.P. writes, "The leading lights of our age often claim to champion the rights of women, and in certain respects the claim is legitimate. At the same time, however, our age has clearly not sought to protect and foster the sacred dignity of women. On the contrary, society would have us remove our wedding garment, divest ourselves of Christ, and put on the 'old man' and make ample provision for the flesh. Men are practically encouraged to treat women as mere objects of pleasure, and women are encouraged to seek this degrading form of attention and accept it as normal and compatible with their dignity."

I began by writing that lust is one of Satan's most effective weapons. Why? According to St. Thomas Aquinas, the daughters (consequences) of lust are "blindness of mind, thoughtlessness, inconstancy, rashness, self-love, hatred of God, love of this world, and abhorrence or despair of a future world." While mortal sin kills the life of grace within us, lust accomplishes this in a most effective way. In essence, it has taken men

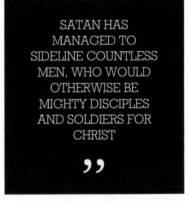

SATAN HAS MANAGED TO SIDELINE COUNTLESS MEN, WHO WOULD OTHERWISE BE MIGHTY DISCIPLES AND SOLDIERS FOR CHRIST

(especially) off the battlefield of spiritual warfare. Instead, they lose any resolve to seek God and His will. They become, in essence, a lump of self-absorbed clay, easily manipulated by the devil. They are lifeless. Satan has managed to sideline countless men, who would otherwise be mighty disciples and soldiers for Christ. Imagine how daunting Christ's army would be if it weren't for millions of souls who have, literally, no desire to enter the fray.

Many are caught in the vice of lust. "Vice" indicates the habitual nature of the sin. This vice reveals the "quality" of a man's soul. Caught in the vice of lust, many confess the sin with little or no resolution to cease its repetition. Therefore, grace may not be given entrance to such a soul while the "daughters of lust" maintain their residence there.

I'm often asked what someone caught in the vice of lust can do. Of course, there are organizations and support groups available. But I often tell men that they need to change their perspective.

This is something I wrote that, I believe, gets to the heart of this proper perspective:

"God's glorious creation began with things such as dirt, then vegetation, then animals, etc. ... it just kept getting better and better. God then created His great love interest ... His adopted children ... human beings. Yet man was created only second to last. Woman is the crescendo ... the last and greatest of all of God's creation! More than a beautiful sunset or starry night or any cascading waterfalls or picturesque mountain range ... God has created nothing more beautiful, more loving, more tender-hearted, more nurturing. That is why women are perfectly positioned to be wife and mother. And, because women are the pinnacle of all God's creations, they too, like the Blessed Mother, should be esteemed as sacred. They have been given the special role of being the tabernacle of God's next love interest."

This is the perspective we must recover. I tell men, "go ahead and notice the wonder of woman – it's not dirty or sinful to do so – and give praise to God, but do that in a split second, and don't entertain the base thoughts of the 'old man.'" I recall when this perspective was prevalent, as I watched in my childhood years, gentlemen stand when a lady entered the room. Oh, how I wish that practice would return!

Prayer of Reparation

My Lord and my God, we have allowed the temptation of the devil to move our hearts to lust and sins of the flesh. We have allowed the desire to deaden our hearts to You and Your will for our lives. We have been too easily led by the accepted morals of the world that have given us supposed permission to indulge the flesh. In our weakness, we have allowed the ancient foe to advance. We turn to You Lord, in our sorrow and guilt, and beg Your forgiveness for our lack of resolve to put on the new man and curb our base desires to indulge the flesh. We beg for the grace of Your goodness to build up within us the strength and endurance You exhibited on the Cross. We know, Lord, if You will it, it will be done. Trusting in You, we offer our prayer to You who live and reign forever. Amen.

Prayer of Exorcism

Lord God of heaven and earth, in Your power and goodness, You created all things. You set a path for us to walk on and a way to an eternal relationship. By the strength of Your arm and Word of Your mouth, cast from Your Holy Church every fearful deceit of the devil. Drive from us manifestations of the demonic that oppress us and beckon us to lust and sins of the flesh. Still the lying tongue of the devil and his forces so that we may act freely and faithfully to Your will. Send Your holy angels to cast out all influence that the demonic entities in charge of lust have planted in Your Church. Free us, our families, our parish, our diocese, and our country from all trickery and deceit perpetrated by the devil and his hellish legions. Trusting in Your goodness Lord, we know if You will it, it will be done, in unity with Your Son and the Holy Spirit, one God forever and ever. Amen.

♤ DAY 11 CHECKLIST ♤

__ Prayer for Freedom from the Devil - pg. 255

__ Daily reflection and prayers

__ Litany of the day – pg. 256

__ Pray a Rosary (intention: exorcism of lust) – pg.275

__ Divine Mercy Chaplet (in reparation for: sin due to lust) – pg. 279

__ Spiritual or corporal work of mercy (see pg. 254)

__ Fast/abstain (according to level)

__ Exercise (according to level/ability)

__ Refrain from conventional media (only 1 hr. of social)

__ Examination of conscience (confession 1x this week)

Day 12

Freedom from
STINGINESS/MISERLINESS

By FR. JAMES ALTMAN

Dear family, who is the one person that most often comes to mind when we think of stingy misers? For many it may be the infamous Ebenezer Scrooge, from Charles Dickens' 1843 novella, *A Christmas Carol.* At the beginning of the story, Scrooge is a cold-hearted miser who despises Christmas. His attitude can be summed up in two words: "Bah, humbug!" Dickens describes Scrooge as "a squeezing, wrenching, grasping, scraping, clutching, covetous, old sinner! Hard and sharp as flint ... secret, and self-contained, and solitary as an oyster." Yes, that about sums up the image we have when we see Scrooge's heartless attitude toward his clerk, Bob Cratchit, whose household includes the crippled child, Tiny Tim.

Maybe you, like me, have run into some Scrooges in your lifetime – miserly people who are stingy with their money like Ebenezer Scrooge. The adjective miserly evolved from the Latin word *miser,* which means "unhappy, wretched." How often do we see unhappiness and wretchedness in the genuinely stingy and miserly?

Why are the stingy and miserly unhappy and wretched? Because misers are a step beyond mere frugality. They are a leap beyond mere prudence in spending. Misers are those who love the accumulation of money, which brings them into direct conflict with the first commandment, to love God above all things.

Jesus directly taught us on this very issue in a parable entitled The Rich Fool, emphasis on the word "fool": "There was a rich man whose land produced a bountiful harvest. He asked himself, 'What shall I do, for I do not have space to store my harvest?' And he said, 'This is what I shall do: I shall tear down my barns and build larger ones. There I shall store all my grain and other goods and I shall say to myself, 'Now as for you, you have so many good things stored up for many years, rest, eat, drink, be merry!'" But God said to him, 'You fool, this night your life will be demanded of you; and the things you have prepared, to whom will they belong?' Thus will it be for the one who stores up treasure for himself but is not rich in what matters to God" (Luke 12:16-21).

Perhaps it was grace that inspired Dickens to write *The Christmas Carol* – grace that enabled him to understand that we are formed by our experiences, but all is not lost. It is not too late; it is never too late, to change. The actual novella opens with a description of Scrooge's lonely and unhappy childhood, and his aspiration for money to avoid poverty. Unlike the rich fool, Scrooge indeed overcame his early formation and, as we know, when he did there was joy: "I don't know what to do! I am as light as a feather, I am as happy as an angel, I am as merry as a school-boy. I am as giddy as a drunken man. A merry Christmas to everybody! A happy New Year to all the world! Hallo here! Whoop! Hallo!"

It is not likely that our own transformation from stinginess and miserliness will arise from being visited by three ghosts, Past, Present, and Future; however, we do not need nocturnal visits from ghosts to effect a change in ourselves. Rather, if we are open to it, we may make the effort to ponder our own past experiences, then meditate upon how these experiences have formed us and resulted in our present, and then make a firm purpose to amend our future, an amendment to be less stingy and miserly with anything we have.

Certainly this applies to any material goods, but perhaps most importantly to our time – time we could spend in prayer of thanksgiving, intercession for others, even imploring God on our own behalf. Indeed, what may be most required of us is our time; it so often is a lot easier to just throw some money at a problem, but extremely difficult to spend some personal time fixing it.

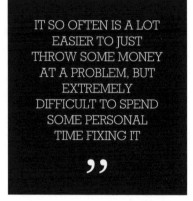

IT SO OFTEN IS A LOT EASIER TO JUST THROW SOME MONEY AT A PROBLEM, BUT EXTREMELY DIFFICULT TO SPEND SOME PERSONAL TIME FIXING IT

"

How stingy and miserly we are with our time. How little we comprehend the implications of the words God spoke to the rich fool: "this night your life will be demanded of you."

Dear family, we must examine our lives. As the great Socrates is said to have uttered: "The unexamined life is not worth living" (as described in *Plato's Apology*, which is a recollection of the speech Socrates gave at his trial. (38a5–6)). One commentator described the meaning of Socrates' statement thusly: "It means any life which is not checkmated, unaccountable is not worth living. It tries to emphasize that everyone has to live a life that they should be proud of, a life that they can look back to what they achieved and say yes indeed I made a mark or I have not lived up to my expectations, so I need to make amends."

We must examine our lives and when we do, let us keep in mind the sobering words of the ghost of Jacob Marley: "'I wear the chain I forged in life,' replied the Ghost, 'I made it link by link, and yard by yard.'" And when we examine our lives let us understand the truth spoken by Scrooge after the visit of the ghost of the Future: "Are these the shadows of the things that Will be, or are they shadows of things that May be, only?" In other words, Scrooge asked it if was too late to change. No, dear family, it is not too late, it is never too late, to change.

Scrooge changed because the three ghosts forced him to examine his life. Let us force ourselves to do the same. After all, that is the whole point of the Examination of Conscience we are supposed to do before entering the Sacrament of Reconciliation. In that examination, let us ask ourselves if we truly love God above all things, or whether we are stingy and miserly with any or many of the gifts God has given us, especially the gift of time. Let us not fear such an examination, but rather revel in the fact that we know transformative grace will come to us through the sacrament. Let us pray that through this transformation it may be said of us as it was said of Scrooge in some concluding words of *A Christmas Carol*: "And it was always said of him, that he knew how to keep Christmas well, if any man alive possessed the knowledge. May that be truly said of us, and all of us!'"

Prayer of Reparation

My Lord and my God, we have allowed the temptation of the devil to move our hearts toward stinginess and miserliness. We have fallen into stinginess and miserliness when we have not lived up to the call of our baptism by not giving back to You a just tithing of our wealth of time, talents, and treasure. We cling to things so much, forgetting the truth that "we can't take it with us." We ignore the words of the great Job: "Naked I came forth from my mother's womb, and naked shall I go back there. The LORD gave and the LORD has taken away; blessed be the name of the LORD!" (Job 1:21). In our weakness, we have been weak in faith and clung to our wealth like the rich fool. In so many ways, we fear the loss of temporal wealth more than we fear the loss of heaven. We turn to You Lord, in our weakness, and beg Your forgiveness for our stinginess and miserliness. We love You Lord, and we beg for the courage to live out the generosity of the Psalmist: "How can I repay the LORD for all the great good done for me? I will raise the cup of salvation and call on the name of the LORD. I will pay my vows to the LORD in the presence of all his people" (Psalm 116:12-14). We know Lord, if You will it, it will be done. Trusting in You, we offer our prayer to You who live and reign forever and ever. Amen.

Prayer of Exorcism

Lord God of heaven and earth, in Your power and goodness, You created all things. You set a path for us to walk on and a way to an eternal relationship. By the strength of Your arm and Word of Your mouth, cast from Your Holy Church every fearful deceit of the devil. Drive from us manifestations of the demonic that oppress us and beckon us to stinginess and miserliness. Still the lying tongue of the devil and his forces so that we may act freely and faithfully to Your will. Send Your holy angels to cast out all influence that the demonic entities in charge of stinginess and miserliness have planted in Your Church. Free us, our families, our parish, our diocese, and our country from all trickery and deceit perpetrated by the devil and his hellish legions. Trusting in Your goodness Lord, we know if You will it, it will be done, in unity with Your Son and the Holy Spirit, one God, forever and ever. Amen.

🔔 DAY 12 CHECKLIST 🔔

___ Prayer for Freedom from the Devil - pg. 255

___ Daily reflection and prayers

___ Litany of the day – pg. 256

___ Pray a Rosary (intention: exorcism of stinginess/miserliness) – pg.275

___ Divine Mercy Chaplet (in reparation for: sin due to stinginess/miserliness) – pg. 279

___ Spiritual or corporal work of mercy (see pg. 254)

___ Fast/abstain (according to level)

___ Exercise (according to level/ability)

___ Refrain from conventional media (only 1 hr. of social)

___ Examination of conscience (confession 1x this week)

Day 13
Freedom from PORNOGRAPHY
By FR. WILLIAM PECKMAN

In 79 A.D., the Roman cities of Pompeii and Herculaneum were buried under the ash of the eruption of Mt. Vesuvius. In the mid-1700s, when the cities were discovered and excavated, we got a good look into life in the earliest days of the spread of Christianity and the culture they were up against. In the ruins were many indications of pornography in brothels and even common homes. The sexual promiscuity of the Roman culture was no secret even if the practice of it was kept behind closed doors in the name of being discreet. How much it saturated the society was a bit of a shock.

Pornography has been with humanity for an exceptionally long time. The word comes from the Greek words *porne* (prostitute) and *graphos* (to write). Prostitution deliberately cheapens the human dignity of a person by exploiting them for sexual gratification; pornography further cheapens that dignity by reducing the person to nothing more than an image with which to self-pleasure.

In 1953, we saw the eventual mainstreaming of pornography with the playboy mentality of Hugh Hefner. Within 50 years, the acceptability of pornography had grown so much that viewing it became seen as both a healthy and normal behavior. It is now a 97-billion-dollar industry that fuels human trafficking worldwide. It is estimated that the sex trafficking trade claims 4.5 million men, women, and children as its victims. These victims are shown pornography to learn how to "perform," and are forced to be a pawn in its production. The consumer in this evil exchange is conditioned to completely objectify the human person as a means of self-gratification. There are fewer more potent cancers in our society today than pornography.

It is legion in our society. Both in soft and hard-core versions (everything from "romance" novels to violence), it permeates the entertainment industry at all levels. It is sung about in music, lauded on TV and in motion pictures as normal guy behavior, and now, with the help of the internet and social media, has spread to the point where our children are taking nude pictures of themselves and sending it to others via texting. It influences how we dress, what we show, and the way we interact. It does permanent damage to the human brain, especially if the person starts using it in adolescence. It is known to inhibit the ability to participate in healthy adult relationships. It is estimated that even among Christians, 64% of men use pornography. In a study done on human sex trafficking, it was remarked that pornography is the gateway to prostitution.

The issue with pornography is that it reduces sex to something outside of the marital bond. It is easy adultery. It divorces sex from the marriage and trains married users how to objectify each other for physical gratification. The grim reality with porn is that it is a total rejection of God's plan for human sexuality. As the U.S. bishops wrote in their 2015 pastoral letter "Create a Clean Heart in Me," deliberately viewing pornography is a grave sin against chastity. Sexual intimacy and the pleasure that derives from it are gifts from God and should remain personal and private, enjoyed within the sacred bond of marriage alone. Such intimacy should not be put on display or be watched by any other person, even if that person is one's own spouse. Nor should the human body be unveiled or treated in a way that objectifies it sexually and reduces it to an erotic stimulant. Jesus is clear in his teaching that sexual immorality is not only a matter of one's actions, but also a matter of one's heart: "You have heard that it was said, 'you shall not commit adultery.' But I say to you, everyone who looks at a woman with lust has already committed adultery with her in his heart" (Matthew 5:27-28).

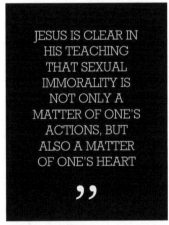

JESUS IS CLEAR IN HIS TEACHING THAT SEXUAL IMMORALITY IS NOT ONLY A MATTER OF ONE'S ACTIONS, BUT ALSO A MATTER OF ONE'S HEART

Pornography is likewise a grave sin against human dignity. As the *Catechism* says, "filming or taking pictures of the intimate parts of the body or of sexual acts does 'grave injury' to the person(s) 'performing,' to anyone responsible for its making or production, and to the public." Pornography dehumanizes the persons depicted, making them into objects of use. Those who produce and distribute pornography harm the common good by encouraging and even causing others to sin. They do serious harm to the women and men who consent to be in pornographic material, often out of desperation for money or out of an impoverished sense of self-worth. Even worse, in some cases pornographers take advantage of those who cannot even give consent – children and other victims of human trafficking – which is both a grave sin and a heinous crime."

Pornography in its variety of forms (print, movie, virtual, TV, music) must be purged from a faithful Catholic's home. It must be treated as the voracious cancer it is. It may well be with us from antiquity, but its influence must be curtailed so that a renewed respect for the human person's dignity and integrity may be restored.

Prayer of Reparation

My Lord and my God, we have allowed the temptation of the devil to move our hearts to objectify our fellow man as a means for self-gratification. We have stilled our hearts to the suffering of those who are filmed. We have been too fearful to stand out in our culture, allowing the scorn of the world to quiet us in our defense of human dignity and chastity. In our fear, we have allowed the ancient foe to advance. We turn to You Lord, in our sorrow and guilt, and beg Your forgiveness for our use of pornography in all its forms. We beg for the grace of Your goodness to build up within us what You sought to build up in Your apostles in that tempest-tossed boat. We know, Lord, if You will it, it will be done. Trusting in You, we offer our prayer to You who live and reign forever. Amen.

Prayer of Exorcism

Lord God of heaven and earth, in Your power and goodness, You created all things. You set a path for us to walk on and a way to an eternal relationship. By the strength of Your arm and Word of Your mouth, cast from Your Holy Church every fearful deceit of the devil. Drive from us manifestations of the demonic that oppress us and beckon us to the use of pornography. Still the lying tongue of the devil and his forces so that we may act freely and faithfully to Your will. Send Your holy angels to cast out all influence that the demonic entities in charge of pornography have planted in Your Church. Free us, our families, our parish, our diocese, and our country from all trickery and deceit perpetrated by the devil and his hellish legions. Trusting in Your goodness Lord, we know if You will it, it will be done, in unity with Your Son and the Holy Spirit, one God forever and ever. Amen.

🔔 DAY 13 CHECKLIST 🔔

__ Prayer for Freedom from the Devil - pg. 255

__ Daily reflection and prayers

__ Litany of the day – pg. 256

__ Pray a Rosary (intention: exorcism of pornography) – pg.275

__ Divine Mercy Chaplet (in reparation for: sin due to pornography) – pg. 279

__ Spiritual or corporal work of mercy (see pg. 254)

__ Fast/abstain (according to level)

__ Exercise (according to level/ability)

__ Refrain from conventional media (only 1 hr. of social)

__ Examination of conscience (confession 1x this week)

Day 14

Freedom from REBELLION

By FR. RICHARD HEILMAN

Recently, I have been pointing to one of Venerable Fulton Sheen's popular TV shows from the 1960s. Sheen entitled this episode, "*Quo Vadis, America*," which translates to "America, Where Are You Going?" This is a reference to a conversation recounted in the apocryphal Acts of Peter in which Peter, fleeing his ministry and the threat of crucifixion in Rome, meets the risen Jesus on the road. Peter asks Jesus "Quo Vadis, Domine?" (Where are You going, Lord?), to which Jesus responds that he is going to Rome to be crucified again. This gives Peter the courage to return to his ministry in Rome, where he ultimately ends up crucified upside down.

This sets up Sheen's talk about patriotism. Sheen said, "Patriotism is a virtue that was allied to the old virtue of the Greeks and Latin called *pietas*, meaning love of God, love of neighbor, love of country. And when one goes out, all go out. When we no longer have love of God, we no longer have love of country."

Sheen continued, "We started our country with a revolution. Revolution is in the air today. In fact, the arguments, today, are that we started that way, why not continue it? We do live in America with a revolutionary tradition. But the question is, what kind of revolution should we have?"

He then tells the story of a soldier who fought at Concord. The soldier was asked why he fought, why he went to Concord. The answer came, "For one reason, that we might govern ourselves." Sheen goes on to say, "Now, what's the revolution of today? VIOLENCE! Violence just for the sake of violence … the new type of revolt, which involves the destruction of everything in the past. And these people who are actuating violence today, claim they are in line with the American Revolution. THEY ARE NOT!"

The point Venerable Fulton Sheen makes is that our

…OUR RIGHTS AND LIBERTIES COME FROM GOD

nation was founded, and has thrived, by the understanding that our rights and liberties come from God. The revolution he was viewing in the 1960s, and we are seeing reenacted today, is a rejection of God, in favor of man.

According to the *Catechism of the Catholic Church*, "The Church teaches … the devil and the other demons were indeed created naturally good by God, but they became evil by their own doing. Scripture speaks of a sin of these angels. This 'fall' consists in the free choice of these created spirits, who radically and irrevocably rejected God and his reign. We find a reflection of that rebellion in the tempter's words to our first parents: 'You will be like God.'"

You see? Once we rebel against God and his reign, we are left to make ourselves our own gods. We are then left to the inevitable outcome, which is totalitarianism. Totalitarianism is a form of government that theoretically permits no individual freedom and that seeks to subordinate all aspects of individual life to the authority of the state. The evil elites, throughout history, have sought such a government. Once they have gained control of every source of influence (media, education system, etc.) they are then equipped to build their army of useful idiots. "Useful idiot" is a derogatory term, referenced in writings of totalitarian governments, for a person perceived as propagandizing for a cause without fully comprehending the cause's goals, and who is cynically used by the cause's leaders.

The evil elites of history have always rebelled against God and country with the same method of operation, which is to use a compliant, violent mob to usher in their plan for totalitarian rule. Sheen puts it this way, "Their principle was that in order to get people to pass through a certain door, there was only one way to do it, and that was the way of terror." There is a reason why there is a "silent majority" ... they're terrified to go against the agenda of the evil elites, and their violent mob.

Venerable Fulton Sheen then brings us to his point: "The world is built on order. There's a plan. So, scientists are able to discover the laws of the universe. And in discovering the laws of the universe, men find harmony. This harmony, and order, had to come from somewhere. It came from God. What is the essence of Satanism? The essence of Satanism is the destruction of that order – the order of law, the order of morality, the order of religion, the order of ethics, anything you please."

This may not be Concord, but the demonic rebellion against God and his beautiful order – against life, liberty, and the pursuit of happiness – is very possibly as severe as it has ever been. *Quo vadis, America?* ... Where are you going, America?

Prayer of Reparation

My Lord and my God, we have allowed the temptation of the devil to move our hearts toward fearfully allowing our nation to rebel against You and Your will. We have fallen into this nationwide rebellion against You when we have not lived up to the call of our baptism by standing against the aggressors of violence and destruction. Instead, like Peter, we flee. We have been too easily swayed by the threats of the elites and their compliant mob to build up a patriotism that is filled with love for You, love of our neighbor, and love of our country. In our weakness, we have allowed the ancient foe to advance. We turn to You Lord, in our sorrow and guilt, and beg Your forgiveness for our lack of resolve to let the visible light of our love for God and country push out the darkness of the rebels. We beg for the grace of Your goodness to build up within us the strength and endurance be this visible light of love for all to see. We know, Lord, if You will it, it will be done. Trusting in You, we offer our prayer to You who live and reign forever and ever. Amen.

Prayer of Exorcism

Lord God of heaven and earth, in Your power and goodness, You created all things. You set a path for us to walk on and a way to an eternal relationship. By the strength of Your arm and Word of Your mouth, cast from Your Holy Church every fearful deceit of the devil. Drive from us manifestations of the demonic that oppress us and beckon us to rebellion. Still the lying tongue of the devil and his forces so that we may act freely and faithfully to do Your will. Send Your holy angels to cast out all influence that the demonic entities in charge of rebellion have planted in Your Church. Free us, our families, our parish, our diocese, and our country from all trickery and deceit perpetrated by the devil and his hellish legions. Trusting in Your goodness Lord, we know if You will it, it will be done, in unity with Your Son and the Holy Spirit, one God forever and ever. Amen.

🔔 DAY 14 CHECKLIST 🔔

__ Prayer for Freedom from the Devil - pg. 255

__ Daily reflection and prayers

__ Litany of the day – pg. 256

__ Pray a Rosary (intention: exorcism of rebellion) – pg.275

__ Divine Mercy Chaplet (in reparation for: sin due to rebellion) – pg. 279

__ Spiritual or corporal work of mercy (see pg. 254)

__ Fast/abstain (according to level)

__ Exercise (according to level/ability)

__ Refrain from conventional media (only 1 hr. of social)

__ Examination of conscience (confession 1x this week)

Day 15
Freedom from WASTEFULNESS
By FR. JAMES ALTMAN

Dear family, maybe you, like me, would hear your mom say something to the effect, "Finish what's on your plate, don't waste it, you know there are people starving in Africa." It's safe to say that when it came to peas and carrots, I was not much concerned about who might be starving. Frankly, if they were hungry, I gladly would have shared my excess peas and carrots.

The same anti-wastefulness doctrine would be drilled in many ways, "Quit standing there with the refrigerator door open" – "Close the door, we're not heating the outside" – "Don't waste your money on that." Whatever it might be, we came to understand that wastefulness was a bad thing. In these "green" times, the culture really has hammered us with wasting any natural resources.

Further, depending on the gravity of what was wasted, the consequences could be great indeed. If we failed to work hard in school, we will have "wasted" our opportunity to get a good education. If we failed to further God-given talents in any other field, like music or sports, we might hear, "What a waste." Pope St. John Paul II said, "Artistic talent is a gift from God and whoever discovers it in himself has a certain obligation: to know that he cannot waste this talent, but must develop it."

If we failed to take advantage of any opportunity for such development, it would be an opportunity "wasted."

Who among us would want to bear the brunt of the accusation, "What a waste"? Jesus the Lord taught about wasting talents in the Parable of the Talents, and we all know what became of the guy who buried his talents in the back yard: "Throw this useless servant into the darkness outside, where there will be wailing and grinding of teeth" (Matthew 25:30).

Ironically, when I was younger, there was a phrase bantered about, essentially as a badge of honor, "I got wasted," when referring to having done some hard partying. Somehow "getting wasted" was a good thing. To my shock, when researching the theology of waste, one search turned up the following: "Guidance on Cannabis Waste Management Requirements." Seriously? What's this world coming to?

Dear family, we all know we are supposed to eat our food, conserve energy, take good care of our bodies, and make something of the talents God has given us. We probably all do a credible job at not being wasteful in those departments. Rather, at the Last Judgment, the thing that likely will be the downfall of many is something few people even think about: wasted time. Victor Hugo, author of *Les Miserables* and *The Hunchback of Notre Dame*, said: "Short as life is, we make it still shorter by the careless waste of time." Unfortunately, it seems not many pay attention to this waste of time until they run out of time. We all have heard the line: "On their deathbed nobody ever says I wish I would have spent another day in the office!" What I never have heard anyone say is "I wish I would have spent another day in church."

So much of our thought processes about waste, maybe all of them, consider waste only as regards to temporal things. Do we ever consider waste regarding preparation for eternity? How much time do we waste that better could be spent in prayer and contemplation of eternal truths upon which our salvation actually depends? Perhaps if we spent more time in prayer and contemplation, we would not feel so great a need to waste so much time immersed in activities that do not promote an increase of grace in our lives. Perhaps we would not waste so much time on the accumulation and maintenance of temporal goods and spend a lot more time in accumulation and maintenance of spiritual goods. Unfortunately, sometimes trying to tell someone this is like "talking to the wall," as the saying goes. In other words, it may seem like "you're wasting your breath!"

St. Vincent de Paul said, "Our business is to attain heaven; everything else is a sheer waste of time." That pretty much says it all. How many of us devote even a small portion of time, much less spend adequate and sufficient time, on the business of attaining heaven? How many of us hear and follow the voice of the Good Shepherd Himself who told us point blank, "When (Jesus) returned to His disciples He found them asleep. He said to Peter, 'So you could not keep watch with Me for one hour? Watch and pray that you may not undergo the test'" (Matthew 26:40-41).

Do we not know that the time for testing is upon us?! Are we even attempting to waste less time on frivolous and temporal matters and spend more time on the only thing that counts?

Even this thought does not give us the fullness of our calling, our duty of service to others. All of us are called to suffer for others, to suffer for their souls. That is why the great Archbishop Sheen said, "Much suffering in hospitals is wasted." It is why Mother Angelica said, "Suffering in itself does not make us holy. It is only when we unite it, out of love, to the suffering of Christ that it has meaning. Suffering without love is wasted pain." It is why Pope St. John Paul II said, "each man, in his suffering, can also become a sharer in the redemptive suffering of Christ."

Dear family, time is the only thing we cannot buy. No amount of money can perpetually delay our inevitable

suffering and death. When that time comes for all of us, we will be called to account for our time. Did we waste it, or did we make good use of it? Did we take the toughest times of suffering and offer it up to share in the redemptive suffering of Christ? Let us once again stop and ponder those ultimate words of St. Vincent de Paul, "Our business is to attain heaven; everything else is a sheer waste of time."

Prayer of Reparation

My Lord and my God, we have allowed the temptation of the devil to move our hearts toward a gross waste of time. We have fallen into countless and endless distractions when we have not lived up to the call of our baptism by not giving back to You a just tithing of our time. We cling to so many meaningless distractions that fill up our day, leaving little energy to spend time with You. In our weakness, we have been weak in faith, and clung to our time as if it were our own, even to the point of acting like the rich fool who himself did not realize: "his time was up." Why is it we are afraid to come to You in time, so we can be with You in eternity? We turn to You Lord, in our weakness, and beg Your forgiveness for our selfish waste of the time You have given us. We love You, Lord, and we beg for the courage to live out our lives giving generously to You of our time, especially our time in suffering, as St. Paul urged us to do: "Watch carefully then how you live, not as foolish persons but as wise, making the most of the opportunity, because the days are evil" (Ephesians 5:15-16). We know, Lord, if You will it, it will be done. Trusting in You, we offer our prayer to You who live and reign forever and ever. Amen.

Prayer of Exorcism

Lord God of heaven and earth, in Your power and goodness, You created all things. You set a path for us to walk on and a way to an eternal relationship. By the strength of Your arm and Word of Your mouth, cast from

Your Holy Church every fearful deceit of the devil. Drive from us manifestations of the demonic that oppress us and beckon us to wastefulness. Still the lying tongue of the devil and his forces so that we may act freely and faithfully to Your will. Send Your holy angels to cast out all influence that the demonic entities in charge of wastefulness have planted in Your Church. Free us, our families, our parish, our diocese, and our country from all trickery and deceit perpetrated by the devil and his hellish legions. Trusting in Your goodness Lord, we know if You will it, it will be done, in unity with Your Son and the Holy Spirit, one God forever and ever. Amen

🔔 DAY 15 CHECKLIST 🔔

__ Prayer for Freedom from the Devil - pg. 255

__ Daily reflection and prayers

__ Litany of the day – pg. 256

__ Pray a Rosary (intention: exorcism of wastefulness) – pg.275

__ Divine Mercy Chaplet (in reparation for: sin due to wastefulness) – pg. 279

__ Spiritual or corporal work of mercy (see pg. 254)

__ Fast/abstain (according to level)

__ Exercise (according to level/ability)

__ Refrain from conventional media (only 1 hr. of social)

__ Examination of conscience (confession 1x this week)

Day 16
Freedom from GODLESSNESS
By FR. WILLIAM PECKMAN

I have a confession. For about four to five years of my life, I was an agnostic. I was so troubled by what I saw in the seminary in the 1980s that I could no longer believe that there was a personal God. I could not believe that He had any concern nor hold on what was happening in the world or even in His own Church. Consequently, I found that nature abhors a vacuum. Something or someone would have to fill that hole in my soul, and someone was going to have to be the judge of morality and the direction of my life. The first problem I tried to fill with pleasure, money, power, and honor. It was an exercise in futility that left me often exhausted and frustrated. The second problem was quite the narcotic: I could decide for myself what was good and evil. Amazingly, such power led to me living a less than chaste life. I was not horrible because the foundation my parents built led me to have a work ethic, to try to be honest, and to avoid substance abuse. I was reduced to a moral pagan. Truth be told, I felt I was living a more moral life than what I had seen in the seminary.

I do not tell you this, kind reader, so that you may think one way or the other about me, only to assure you I know this sin from its maddening and intoxicating inside.

Our society is largely agnostic and atheistic. Our civil religion tips its hat in God's general direction occasionally but largely resents any influence religion, particularly

Judeo-Christianity, has in the public purview. God has been chased from the public square, from our schools, and from our day to day lives. There are forms of politics such as socialism and Marxism that are expressly atheistic. They must be for the state takes the place of all authority and is the giver of all rights. We can't have a deity interfering with that!

There are many within the Church, even among her leaders, who are agnostic or atheistic, either practically or by confession. I would posit that it is impossible for some within the Church who have engaged in nefarious and predatory behavior to do such and believe anything of Jesus Christ or a personal God. Certainly, the pervasive watering down of catechesis would point to a de facto agnosticism among so many academics. You see, nature does abhor a vacuum, and if we divorce the idea of a personal and transcendent God from religion, all we have left is a social justice not-for-profit with arcane rituals and occasion statuary.

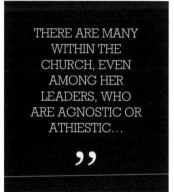

THERE ARE MANY WITHIN THE CHURCH, EVEN AMONG HER LEADERS, WHO ARE AGNOSTIC OR ATHIESTIC...

"

In Eden, the devil grounds his temptation in a belief that God does not want what is good for us. In this, he can tempt us to become our own gods, knowing for ourselves what is good and evil. He can sow vast amounts of seeds of doubt by just showing us the evil others do; especially the evil done by those who claim to represent God. The last 100+ years have been a field day for the devil to sow such seed!

To combat such a virulent temptation, we must cultivate the theological virtue of faith. This is more than making professions of faith or intellectually adopting points of the teachings of the Church. It is adopting these teachings in our lives and allowing them to draw us closer to God. We will have to do this during a storm! We will have to do this even when we see immense scandal in our Church and frightening godlessness in society. This allows us to give proper Christian witness to those scandalized or seeking. It allows others to see Christ through us.

One of the main reasons I returned to the Catholic faith and back into the seminary and priesthood, despite many misgivings, was that complaining about the poor witness and scandalous behavior of some within the Church did not absolve me of following the vocational path God had beckoned me to. I had a responsibility to live the type of life Christ calls us to live, authentically and powerfully. While I completely understand the reasons why people wander away or outright flee from the Church, I also understand that trying to fill the God-shaped hole in us with the things of this world is a frustrating dead-end; the narcotic of being one's own god leaves you empty and anchorless. Our society is exhibit A in this fool's errand. There is no denying that anger, frustration, and feeling adrift are hallmarks of our society and in so many of our churches.

St. Augustine, in his *Confessions*, reminds us, "Our hearts are restless until they rest in Thee." Let us not let the temptations of the devil leave our hearts wandering and baseless. Let us refute the devil and hold fast to the faith and relationship Christ has in store for us.

Prayer of Reparation

My Lord and my God, we have allowed the temptation of the devil to move our hearts to doubt in Your goodness. We have stilled our tongues in the face of evil. We have been too fearful to stand out in our culture, allowing the strong storms to quell our trust in You. Through our sinfulness and rebellion, we have, at times, been a source of scandal for those searching. In our fear, we have allowed the ancient foe to advance. We turn to You Lord, in our sorrow and guilt, and beg Your forgiveness for our faithlessness and timidity. We beg for the grace of Your goodness to build up within us what You sought to build up in Your apostles in that tempest-tossed boat. We know, Lord, if You will it, it will be done. Trusting in You, we offer our prayer to You who live and reign forever and ever. Amen

Prayer of Exorcism

Lord God of heaven and earth, in Your power and goodness, You created all things. You set a path for us to walk on and a way to an eternal relationship. By the strength of Your arm and Word of Your mouth, cast from Your Holy Church every fearful deceit of the devil. Drive

from us manifestations of the demonic that oppress us and beckon us to faithlessness and disbelief. Still the lying tongue of the devil and his forces so that we may act freely and faithfully to Your will. Send Your holy angels to cast out all influence that the demonic entities in charge of godlessness have planted in Your Church. Free us, our families, our parish, our diocese, and our country from all trickery and deceit perpetrated by the devil and his hellish legions. Trusting in Your goodness Lord, we know if You will it, it will be done, in unity with Your Son and the Holy Spirit, One God forever and ever. Amen.

🔔 DAY 16 CHECKLIST 🔔

__ Prayer for Freedom from the Devil - pg. 255

__ Daily reflection and prayers

__ Litany of the day – pg. 256

__ Pray a Rosary (intention: exorcism of godlessness) – pg.275

__ Divine Mercy Chaplet (in reparation for: sin due to godlessness) – pg. 279

__ Spiritual or corporal work of mercy (see pg. 254)

__ Fast/abstain (according to level)

__ Exercise (according to level/ability)

__ Refrain from conventional media (only 1 hr. of social)

__ Examination of conscience (confession 1x this week)

Day 17
Freedom from LUKEWARMNESS
By FR. RICHARD HEILMAN

In the Book of Revelation, we see the Lord has some rather severe words about the lukewarm: "I know your works; I know that you are neither cold nor hot. I wish you were either cold or hot. So, because you are lukewarm, neither hot nor cold, I will spit you out of My mouth" (Revelation 3:16). Pope St. Pius V went so far as to say, "All the evil in the world is due to lukewarm Catholics." Pope St. Pius X showed no less disdain with, "All the strength of Satan's reign is due to the easygoing weakness of Catholics." Wow! All the evil in the world? All the strength of Satan's reign? Spit you out of My mouth? The level of fury toward the lukewarm is alarming. Why?

Here's why. Let's look at the passage from Revelation. Our Lord, first, wishes we were "hot or cold." It's easy to see why the Lord would wish someone were hot. Someone who is "hot" would be that soul blazing with the "fire of love" for God, with a fiery passion to do His will.

So, why would our Lord wish someone were "cold"? Someone who is cold has completely disconnected from God and can often even be antagonistic toward God. So, why would our Lord wish for that? Because "cold souls," who have outwardly drawn the line in the sand and proclaimed their stance in relation to God, have a greater chance for hitting rock bottom and giving their life over to God; they have a greater chance for conversion.

Furthermore, a soul clearly disconnected from God does little to influence souls that are "hot" from straying away from our Lord, as "cold souls" are seen clearly for who they are and where they stand.

So, why the outrage toward the lukewarm? Because the

lukewarm do the most damage. They are highly effective in modeling for others how to be a very poor or even a "fake" Catholic. While "cold souls" openly disavow any claim to be a faithful Catholic, lukewarm souls make that claim while they betray the Lord at every turn.

Lukewarm souls are those who have allowed their faith to diminish to little more than what appears to be faith in the eyes of man. Lukewarm souls will often "use" their Catholic faith to build their own personal brand. So, you'll often see politicians make the claim of being a devout Catholic while they advocate for a plethora of evil policies that horrify God. Or there are those lukewarm Catholics who see no problem voting these evil politicians into power. This is a-okay for the lukewarm, as they have convinced themselves that God's mercy extends to allowing every kind of sin. Which is why lukewarm souls may go to a communal penance service once or twice a year "to be seen," but really don't see any reason for this sacrament.

The most horrifying thing about lukewarm souls is that they usually possess the sins against the Holy Spirit that are referred to as "unforgiveable."

The unforgiveness is about unrepentance. Lukewarm souls have convinced themselves, and poorly modeled for others, that "they don't need to prove their love for God." In other words, they think they can commit any sin and avoid prayer and any charitable work beyond basic obligations, and their ticket is punched because of "mercy." And, of course, nobody should "judge" anyone, according to the lukewarm soul. St. Thomas Aquinas said, "mercy without justice is the mother of dissolution; justice without mercy is cruelty. To correct the sinner is a work of mercy."

Lukewarm souls are like a dangerous virus that spreads throughout the Church. On issues of human life, sex, marriage, family, faith, and morality, many within the Catholic Church have absolutely no problem advocating for laws, policies, and politicians that clearly oppose the will of God. This "lukewarm virus" has spread so far that as many as 40% of Catholics favor abortion and 61% of Catholics support gay marriage. Now, you can see why our Lord, Pope St. Pius V, and Pope St. Pius X are so outraged by the lukewarm.

To combat the demonic viral spread of lukewarmness, we must cultivate in ourselves the Holy Spirit's gift of fear of the Lord, also known as awe and wonder. Fear of the Lord is the gateway gift to all the gifts of the Holy Spirit. If your local parish is cultivating a watered-down, lukewarm version of Catholicism that avoids Church teaching on any "hot button" issues, "GET OUT!" Or, if possible, work with the pastor to cultivate reverent liturgies, frequent confession, ample opportunities for Adoration of the Blessed Sacrament, and the practice of many devotions. And, for heaven's sake, have your pastor's back when he hits hot-button issues. This all assists the faithful in "drawing nearer unto the Lord." This gives the soul immunity to the virus of lukewarmness.

Prayer of Reparation

My Lord and my God, we have allowed the temptation of the devil to move our hearts toward fearfully allowing the spread of lukewarmness throughout our nation and the Catholic Church. We have fallen into this widespread lukewarmness when we have not lived up to the call of our baptism to, day-by-day, deepen our love and faith in You. We have been too easily swayed by the poor example of the Catholic lukewarm and have held our tongue when a few words of correction could lift them out of their unrepentance and nearer unto You. In our weakness, we have allowed the ancient foe to advance. We turn to You Lord, in our sorrow and guilt, and beg Your forgiveness for any of our own lukewarmness or our lack of resolve to lift souls out of this darkness. We beg for the grace of Your goodness to build up within us the strength and endurance to be this visible light of fervent faith in You. We know, Lord, if You will it, it will be done. Trusting in

You, we offer our prayer to You who live and reign forever and ever. Amen.

Prayer of Exorcism

Lord God of heaven and earth, in Your power and goodness, You created all things. You set a path for us to walk on and a way to an eternal relationship. By the strength of Your arm and Word of Your mouth, cast from Your Holy Church every fearful deceit of the devil. Drive from us manifestations of the demonic that oppress us and beckon us to lukewarmness. Still the lying tongue of the devil and his forces so that we may act freely and faithfully to do Your will. Send Your holy angels to cast out all influence that the demonic entities in charge of lukewarmness have planted in Your Church. Free us, our families, our parish, our diocese, and our country from all trickery and deceit perpetrated by the devil and his hellish legions. Trusting in Your goodness Lord, we know if You will it, it will be done, in unity with Your Son and the Holy Spirit, One God forever and ever. Amen.

♔DAY 17 CHECKLIST♔

__ Prayer for Freedom from the Devil - pg. 255

__ Daily reflection and prayers

__ Litany of the day – pg. 256

__ Pray a Rosary (intention: exorcism of lukewarmness)
   – pg.275

__ Divine Mercy Chaplet (in reparation for: sin due to
   lukewarmness) – pg. 279

__ Spiritual or corporal work of mercy (see pg. 254)

__ Fast/abstain (according to level)

__ Exercise (according to level/ability)

__ Refrain from conventional media (only 1 hr. of social)

__ Examination of conscience (confession 1x this week)

Day 18
Freedom from JEALOUSY
By FR. JAMES ALTMAN

Dear family, let us ponder the root cause of jealousy. It's called being human. From the beginning, humanity has always been susceptible to its grip. Humanity is prone to jealousy because – remember this now, it's so basic and fundamental – nothing ever is enough.

Think of what I call The Life Lesson of Adam and Eve. They lived in paradise! They essentially had everything, and they did not have sickness and death, so they could have enjoyed everything forever! I like this part: they had dominion over the animals. They did not have to fear a lion or a shark. If they were trying to take a nap – I'm sleep deprived, so this is a very meaningful example for me – if they were trying to take a nap and the lion was getting all growly making noise, all they had to do was to tell it to get lost. They. Had. Everything. Except one piddly dumb tree. And yet, having everything wasn't enough. Human nature kicked in. Lucifer understood human nature. What did he do? He tempted Adam and Eve not with more of everything, but only with the one thing.

The same goes for us, dear family. The devil does not come in with a red cape and pointy horns. He comes as everything you ever wished for.

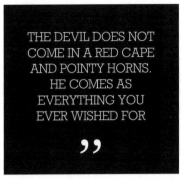

> THE DEVIL DOES NOT COME IN A RED CAPE AND POINTY HORNS. HE COMES AS EVERYTHING YOU EVER WISHED FOR

Here is a true story about human nature from psychology. Fill a room full of toys...chuck full of toys. Then put one kid in the middle of it. Like the proverbial "kid in a candy store," the kid can pick and choose whatever he wants. He's happy. Couldn't be happier. Then … introduce another kid. Put another kid in the room, a second kid. He looks around at all the toys and picks one for himself. What happens? The first kid gets jealous. He thinks along the lines of "I must have not chosen the best one for myself because that kid over there chose that one." Even though the first kid was perfectly happy playing all by himself, when that second kid comes in and chooses a different toy, the first kid just has to have it!

Adam and Eve. Two kids in a toy room. Both have a form of jealousy. The *Cambridge Dictionary* defines jealousy as "a feeling of unhappiness and anger because someone has something or someone that you want." We might readily understand this and apply it to the two kids in the toy room. But what about Adam and Eve? They were jealous of something God had, or at least what Lucifer told them God had.

Remember Lucifer's damnable lie: He asked the woman, "Did God really say, 'You shall not eat from any of the trees in the garden?'" The woman answered the snake: "We may eat of the fruit of the trees in the garden; it is only about the fruit of the tree in the middle of the garden that God said, 'You shall not eat it or even touch it, or else you will die.'" But the snake said to the woman: "You certainly will not die! God knows well that when you eat of it your eyes will be opened and you will be like gods, who know good and evil" (Gen 3:1-5).

How often do such words poison our own thought processes? How often do we turn our eyes away from what we have toward something someone else has? How often do we compare and despair?

Dear family, there is a secret to peace and tranquility. It is easy to say, though perhaps, at times, especially at a time of seeming deprivation, it is hard to do. The secret is this: to be happy, you must be happy for what you do have, and not unhappy for what you do not have.

Our humanity is poisoned by a compulsion to compare and despair. Looking back, at various times I thought I wanted to be a champion tennis player, a very wealthy person, or a rock star, maybe live on some island in the Caribbean. Ultimately the wants came from comparing and despairing over such things as the fact that I was growing up in a snow-belt where the tennis courts were buried for 2/3 of the year. Would I have been happy and content and at peace if I had attained any of those things? No. The Life Lesson of Adam and Eve proves not. Nothing ever is enough. My parents tried to teach this to me, saying such things as "there always will be someone with more ____" – just fill in the blank. Even if we accept this as truth, it still is hard to come to terms with the proposition that someone else has more of something.

There is only one way to overcome jealousy, and that is to discover that God is in love with you. Wholly and completely in love…with you. Yes, yes, we know: "For God so loved the world that He gave His only Son, so that everyone who believes in Him might not perish but might have eternal life" (John 3:16). Nowadays, most people do not even believe in God, much less that He loves them personally, much less that He sent His Divine Son to die for us. So instead, let us focus on another Johannine verse: "And the Word became flesh and made His dwelling among us, and we saw His glory, the glory as of the Father's only Son, full of grace and truth" (John 1:14).

Dear family, St. John, the beloved apostle saw the glory of Jesus, full of grace and truth. That is why he could write to us: "What was from the beginning, what we have heard, what we have seen with our eyes, what we looked upon and touched with our hands concerns the Word of life - for the life was made visible; we have seen it and testify to it and proclaim to you the eternal life that was with the Father and was made visible to us - what we have seen and heard we proclaim now to you, so that you too may have fellowship with us; for our fellowship is with the Father and with his Son, Jesus Christ. We are writing this so that our joy may be complete" (1 John 1:1-4).

Notice, St. John did not say his joy would be complete if he had a new car or a house on the beach. He certainly did not say his joy would be complete if he had dominion over the animals. St. John's joy only would be complete if he shared the glory of Jesus, His Grace, His Truth.

Dear family, that is the only way we ever will be happy. If jealousy pangs strike, understand we are not happy for what we have, but unhappy for what we do not have. But God has given us all we need to be happy…Himself. That is why He came in the first place. To give us that only thing. Himself. So, the next time jealousy rears its ugly, Luciferian head – and that is indeed where jealousy originates – turn your eyes upon Jesus. Turn them upon His Holy Cross. Ponder the infinite love poured out in every drop of blood, in every struggling breath … unto His last drop of blood and His last breath.

Take your eyes off whatever tree Lucifer points you to, whatever forbidden fruit with which he taunts you, and as the hymn goes: "Turn your eyes upon Jesus. Look full in His wonderful face. And the things, the things of earth, will grow strangely dim. In the light of His glory and grace."

Prayer of Reparation

My Lord and my God, we have allowed the temptation of the devil to move our hearts toward jealousy. We compare and despair. We have fallen into countless times of sinful dissatisfaction, when all the gifts You have given us – are never enough. We long for so many meaningless things of earth. We spend so much time working so hard for such meaningless things of earth. And then we discover we still are not satisfied; we still are not happy. We turn to You Lord, in our weakness, and beg Your forgiveness for our jealousy – our desire to have those gifts You have given to other children – for our dissatisfaction with the gifts You have given us. We love You, Lord, and we beg for the courage to live out our lives as St. John wrote so perfectly – that we will find our joy in sharing the joy we find in You, and only You. We know Lord, if You will it, it will be done. Trusting in You, we offer our prayer to You who live and reign forever and ever. Amen.

Prayer of Exorcism

Lord God of heaven and earth, in Your power and goodness, You created all things. You set a path for us to walk on and a way to an eternal relationship. By the strength of Your arm and Word of Your mouth, cast from Your Holy Church every fearful deceit of the devil. Drive from us manifestations of the demonic that oppress us and beckon us to jealousy. Still the lying tongue of the devil and his forces so that we may act freely and faithfully to Your will. Send Your holy angels to cast out all influence that the demonic entities in charge of jealousy have planted in Your Church. Free us, our families, our parish, our diocese, and our country from all trickery and deceit perpetrated by the devil and his hellish legions. Trusting in Your goodness Lord, we know if You will it, it will be done, in unity with Your Son and the Holy Spirit, one God, forever and ever. Amen.

♤ DAY 18 CHECKLIST ♤

___ Prayer for Freedom from the Devil - pg. 255

___ Daily reflection and prayers

___ Litany of the day – pg. 256

___ Pray a Rosary (intention: exorcism of jealousy) – pg.275

___ Divine Mercy Chaplet (in reparation for: sin due to jealousy) – pg. 279

___ Spiritual or corporal work of mercy (see pg. 254)

___ Fast/abstain (according to level)

___ Exercise (according to level/ability)

___ Refrain from conventional media (only 1 hr. of social)

___ Examination of conscience (confession 1x this week)

Day 19
Freedom from SYNCRETISM
By FR. WILLIAM PECKMAN

"Elijah went before the people and said, 'How long will you waver between two opinions? If the Lord is God, follow Him; but if Baal is god, follow him.' But the people said nothing" (1 Kings 18:21).

In the Old Testament, both the Kingdom of Israel and the Kingdom of Judah participated in the same sin. It was a form of idolatry in which the people would worship both the God of Israel and the gods of the surrounding regions. This participation in more than one religion is called syncretism. God likens syncretism, in the Scriptures, to an unfaithful spouse who wants the benefits of life with her spouse while acting the harlot with anyone. On Mt. Carmel, Elijah proposes a test to the Kingdom of Israel. He and the prophets of Baal will prepare a sacrifice without lighting it and the God who answers with fire is to be worshipped alone. He poses the above question to them. Notice they do not answer. I can only imagine the awkward silence felt at that moment.

The southern kingdom of Judah also would worship God up on the temple mount and would go into the Valley of Hinnom (known in Jesus' time as Gehenna) and worship idols, even sacrificing their children to these idols. The prophets, particularly Jeremiah, warn the people that God takes note of such infidelity and will not allow the people to benefit from a relationship with Him while they play the harlot in the valley of Hinnom. For both kingdoms, their sin of syncretism led to their downfall and exile. God will not allow us to keep the benefits of a relationship with Him while we push Him away in favor of our idols.

In Matthew 6:24, Jesus reminds us we cannot serve two masters; that we cannot serve both God and mammon. Notice mammon is not capitalized. It is not an idol per se. Mammon is wealth or any other worldly pursuit we allow to take the number one position that rightly belongs to God. Most church going Catholics would say that they do not worship anyone or anything but God. That reminds me of Jeremiah 2:23, ""How can you say, 'I am not defiled; I have not run after the Baals'? See how you behaved in the valley; consider what you have done." The people do not acknowledge their idolatry under the pretense that they do go to the temple.

Our society has become godless and exerts much pressure to make sure all are like-minded. The third commandment to keep holy the Sabbath is so forgotten as to be rarely practiced. Even Sunday morning has been taken over by sports, shopping, chores, and other things that turn Mass (if one goes at all) into something that is "fit in" instead of 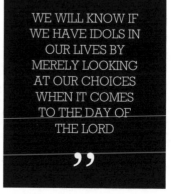 prioritized — as if the day of the Lord is instead the hour

WE WILL KNOW IF WE HAVE IDOLS IN OUR LIVES BY MERELY LOOKING AT OUR CHOICES WHEN IT COMES TO THE DAY OF THE LORD

of the Lord. We will know if we have idols in our lives by merely looking at our choices when it comes to the day of the Lord. Is Mass the center of the day? It is what everything else is scheduled around? Is there rest? Or is the pursuit of honor, pleasure, money, or power more sought after? Chances are if the day of the Lord has been reduced to the hour of the Lord, and if that hour of the Lord is a lesser choice when given other options, than the rest of the week is likely just as godless.

While I do sympathize with those who became distraught at churches closing because of COVID-19, it greatly saddened me that for 65-70% of self-professed Catholics the closing of churches made no difference on what they did with Sunday. The closing of ball fields and stores had a greater impact. Yet, these same self-proclaimed Catholics will expect God's protecting hand and all the benefits of a relationship with Him, while ignoring God and disdaining His sacramental grace in favor of worldly idols and their promised benefits. Perhaps we would do well to look how that worked out for the Kingdoms of Israel and Judah.

Now is the time of Jeremiah! The call to turn our backs on our idols of wealth, honor, power, and pleasure (and that includes our disproportionate and slavish relationship with sports, entertainment, and leisure) and put God back to being our only God and worshipping Him alone. We need to cultivate that virtue of fidelity to God in our lives. The devil will use every distraction, perceived good, selfish desire, and twisted logic to deter us from seeking such fidelity. The devil wants no better for us than the lot he himself is consigned to for eternity. He wants for us the same eternal broken relationship that he has chosen by his own infidelity. He will not warn us of the price of syncretism. He will encourage us to worship anything and everything as more pertinent to our lives than God; he is all too happy to have us treat God as some here-after insurance policy. We must fight him. Hold fast to the faith and relationship Christ has in store for us.

Prayer of Reparation

My Lord and my God, we have allowed the temptation of the devil to move our hearts to not see fulfillment in Your goodness. We have stilled our tongues in the face of evil. We have been too fearful to stand out in our culture, allowing the lure of worldly idols to turn our hearts against you. We have expected You to be pleased with our duplicitous hearts. We have, at times, been a source of scandal for those searching through our sinfulness and rebellion to You. In our fear, we have allowed the ancient foe to advance. We turn to You Lord, in our sorrow and guilt, and beg Your forgiveness for our syncretism and infidelity. We beg for the grace of Your goodness to build up within us what You sought to build up in Your apostles in that tempest-tossed boat. We know, Lord, if You will it, it will be done. Trusting in you, we offer our prayer to You who live and reign forever. Amen.

Prayer of Exorcism

Lord God of heaven and earth, in Your power and goodness, You created all things. You set a path for us to walk on and a way to an eternal relationship. By the strength of Your arm and Word of Your mouth, cast from Your Holy Church every fearful deceit of the devil. Drive from us manifestations of the demonic that oppress us and beckon us to faithlessness and syncretism. Still the lying tongue of the devil and his forces so that we may act freely and faithfully to Your will. Send Your holy angels to cast out all influence that the demonic entities in charge of syncretism have planted in Your Church. Free us, our families, our parish, our diocese, and our country from all trickery and deceit perpetrated by the devil and his hellish legions. Trusting in Your goodness Lord, we know if You will it, it will be done, in unity with Your Son and the Holy Spirit, one God, forever and ever. Amen.

♤ DAY 19 CHECKLIST ♤

__ Prayer for Freedom from the Devil - pg. 255

__ Daily reflection and prayers

__ Litany of the day – pg. 256

__ Pray a Rosary (intention: exorcism of syncretism) –
pg.275

__ Divine Mercy Chaplet (in reparation for: sin due to
syncretism) – pg. 279

__ Spiritual or corporal work of mercy (see pg. 254)

__ Fast/abstain (according to level)

__ Exercise (according to level/ability)

__ Refrain from conventional media (only 1 hr. of social)

__ Examination of conscience (confession 1x this week)

Day 20

Freedom from LACK OF TRUST IN DIVINE PROVIDENCE

By FR. RICHARD HEILMAN

Recently, in the past few years, I lost four priests who were near and dear to me: my uncle and Godfather (the inspiration for my priesthood), my spiritual director, my bishop, and my best friend. These four priests were more than just brothers in Christ, they were my lifeblood. During the many challenges of life, especially those unique to priesthood, these men were kindred spirits to me. Not only did we recognize together, the M.O. (Method of Operation) of Satan in today's world, but we were all in agreement as to the ways God was calling all of us, especially priests, to engage in a counter-offensive against the tactics of the devil.

By and large, we all knew it was incumbent upon us to

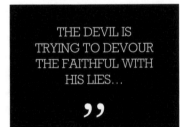

THE DEVIL IS TRYING TO DEVOUR THE FAITHFUL WITH HIS LIES...

"

do all we could to speak the truth, open and honestly, but to do so in the most loving way possible. The devil is trying to devour the faithful with his lies, and we all knew it, and we were all passionate about calling the devil out and leading the faithful to truth. More than anything, as shepherds, we all knew we were called, especially during the time we now live, to do all we could to assist the flock in coming to the place where they cry out, "My Lord and my God!"

Of course, the devil hates, more than anything, truth and reverence. Therefore, Satan works especially hard to destroy anyone who dares to thwart the devil's plan to mislead and confuse souls, as he works diligently to deaden the hearts of the faithful. If we get in his way, he will get busy to take us out. In many respects, this is the reason religious leaders recoil in their call to administer truth and reverence. They have come to understand just how vicious the devil can be, if we dare "go there."

I recall when Bishop Morlino first arrived in our diocese with his passion for "truth and reverence." The assaults on him, especially from those who held the levers of power and influence, were ferociously vicious. This did not deter this courageous bishop in any way. During this time, or whenever the attacks were turned on me, we stuck together in brotherly love.

So many times, I have been tempted to lose trust in God's providence. I mean, here I am, alone on the battlefield, I felt. My four closest "battle buddies" are no longer here. Not only do I miss them, but I feel like I could now be "easy pickins" for the devil to swoop in and take me out, without the security of knowing my battle buddies are right there, ready to in essence, call out, "I got your six" (I got your back).

I share this just to say that I can relate to all those who face devastating challenges in their lives. Yes, I can relate to those who are tempted to lose their trust in God's providence. Sometimes, we want to just say, "What the heck, God?!"

But I didn't say that. Instead, by God's grace, my hope has deepened during this challenging time. According to the *Catechism of the Catholic Church*: "Hope is the theological virtue by which we desire the kingdom of heaven and eternal life as our happiness, placing our trust in Christ's promises and relying not on our own strength, but on the help of the grace of the Holy Spirit" (CCC 1817).

In my case, having lost my battle buddies, I'm thinking about the kingdom of heaven and eternal life as our happiness more than ever before. While my battle buddies are no longer here to support me in the flesh, my relationship with them has only deepened as I know they've "got my six" in an even more powerful way. They are my prayer warriors now! For example, I know we received an amazing new bishop, when it seemed inevitable we would not, only because Bishop Morlino interceded for us.

As we all know, we are facing challenges that are historic. How easy, and seemingly justifiable, it would be for all of us to despair as we lose our trust in God's providence. I choose not to, and I pray it is the same with you. Instead, my prayer has become even more fervent, my resolve to enter the fray against the devil's schemes has become more intensified, and my confidence in the power of God, versus my own power, has become stronger than ever.

I've come to understand that sticking with God and believing and trusting in His providence in challenging times is a lot like resistance training (lifting weights). With the power of God's grace, we "press against" these challenges, and our faith, hope, and love become even stronger. We must trust in God's providence during these storms of our lives and know He will carry us safely to shore. And know that, ultimately, heaven is going to be amazing!

Prayer of Reparation

My Lord and my God, we have allowed the temptation of the devil to move our hearts to not see fulfillment in Your goodness. We have stilled our tongues in the face of evil. We have been too weak to stand against the temptation to lose our trust in Your providence. We have expected You to remove the challenges in our life, and so we have readily doubted You when difficulties enter in. We have, at times, been a source of scandal for those searching through our sinfulness and lack of trust in You. In our fear, we have allowed the ancient foe to advance. We turn to You Lord, in our sorrow and guilt, and beg Your forgiveness for our lack of trust in Your providence. We beg for the grace of Your goodness to build up within us what You sought to build up in Your apostles in that tempest-tossed boat. We know, Lord, if You will it, it will be done. Trusting in You, we offer our prayer to You who live and reign forever. Amen.

Prayer of Exorcism

Lord God of heaven and earth, in Your power and goodness, You created all things. You set a path for us to walk on and a way to an eternal relationship. By the strength of Your arm and Word of Your mouth, cast from Your Holy Church every fearful deceit of the devil. Drive from us manifestations of the demonic that oppress us and beckon us to lack of trust in Your providence. Still the lying tongue of the devil and his forces so that we may act freely and faithfully to Your will. Send Your holy angels to cast out all influence that the demonic entities in charge of doubt have planted in Your Church. Free us, our families, our parish, our diocese, and our country from all trickery and deceit perpetrated by the devil and his hellish legions. Trusting in Your goodness Lord, we know if You will it, it will be done, in unity with Your Son and the Holy Spirit, one God, forever and ever. Amen.

🔔 DAY 20 CHECKLIST 🔔

__ Prayer for Freedom from the Devil - pg. 255

__ Daily reflection and prayers

__ Litany of the day – pg. 256

__ Pray a Rosary (intention: exorcism of lack of trust in divine providence) – pg.275

__ Divine Mercy Chaplet (in reparation for: sin due to lack of trust in divine providence) – pg. 279

__ Spiritual or corporal work of mercy (see pg. 254)

__ Fast/abstain (according to level)

__ Exercise (according to level/ability)

__ Refrain from conventional media (only 1 hr. of social)

__ Examination of conscience (confession 1x this week)

Day 21

Freedom from INDIFFERENCE

By FR. JAMES ALTMAN

Dear family, of all the things you can apply the saying "take it or leave it" to, going deeper into our faith is not one of them. We cannot be indifferent to our faith.

When we try to reflect on some principle of our faith - like "indifference" - it is always good to refer to the *Catechism* to get a working definition, so we all are on the same page. That is my starting point.

So, §2093 states: "Faith in God's love encompasses the call and the obligation to respond with sincere love to divine charity. The first commandment enjoins us to love God above everything and all creatures for Him and because of Him." Ok. So good so far.

Then it follows up with §2094 which states: "One can sin against God's love in various ways" - and then includes the definition for indifference: "indifference neglects or refuses to reflect on divine charity; it fails to consider its prevenient goodness and denies its power."

Oh, dear family, my head hurts when I try to read something like §2094, something someone cannot seem to put in understandable language. If I asked you, "Exactly what does it mean to fail to consider divine charity's prevenient goodness and deny its power?" could you answer the question? Don't feel badly if you couldn't; I couldn't either. I had to look up the word "prevenient" and then try to place it in some sort of context of "goodness,"

132

and then try to figure out how does refusing to reflect on divine charity have anything to do with understanding prevenient goodness and, more so, what that has to do with denying its power? Is it any wonder people do not get through the *Catechism* when they run into roadblocks like this? I say all this just so you know you are not alone. Even priests sometimes struggle with this stuff.

For the record, the definition of prevenient is "preceding in time or order; antecedent." So indifference, which apparently is neglecting to reflect on divine charity, means failing to consider its "preceding in time or order, antecedent" goodness. But what does that even mean?!?

In the law, there is an ongoing movement to take "legalese" - the formal and technical language of legal documents that is often hard to understand - and put it into "plain English." So, let us try to do that here.

God loved us first. His love preceded humanity's creation; it was so great that He willed us into existence so He could share it with us. And then, when we did not reciprocate that love (that's the whole fall of Adam and Eve thing and every sin afterwards), He still loved us so much that He sacrificed His only Son to hopefully inspire us to love Him back. In fact, He sent His Son even though He knew exactly what some of us would do to Him, because He knew it would be proof of His divine love. It is why St. Paul - so cognizant of this infinite love of God - hardly could keep in the immensity of his praise and worship for God when he wrote to the Ephesians: "Praised be the God and Father of our Lord, Jesus Christ, who has bestowed on us in Christ every spiritual blessing in the heavens. God chose us in Him, before the world began, to be holy and blameless in His sight. He predestined us to be His adopted sons through Jesus Christ, such was His will and pleasure, that all might praise the glorious favor He has bestowed on us in His beloved. In Him, and through His blood, we have been redeemed, and our sins forgiven, so immeasurably generous is God's favor to us" (Ephesians 1:3-7).

It is no accident that in the *Breviary*, the Church's Liturgy of the Hours, this passage is prayed every Monday at Evening Prayer. It, along with the entire *Breviary*, is a constant reminder of God's love for us. To pray the Liturgy of the Hours is to contemplate and reflect upon Divine Charity. It is the opposite of indifference.

So maybe by considering the opposite of indifference, we get a better understanding of whether we are or are not indifferent. If we want to know if we have fallen victim to indifference, perhaps the best answer is to ask the question: Do we immerse ourselves daily in contemplating God's love, so much so that we, like St. Paul, are compelled to praise and worship God in such words as he wrote to the Ephesians? Do we reflect enough upon the magnitude of God's love, expressed in our very own existence, such that we are

DO WE IMMERSE OURSELVES DAILY IN CONTEMPLATING GOD'S LOVE....?

,,

compelled to give back to Him even just a tithing of the countless gifts He has given us?

Having just celebrated two Holy Masses of Christian Burial, this thought is fresh in my mind, the words prayed after the final Song of Farewell: "We give You thanks for the blessings which You bestowed upon (decedent) in this life: they are signs to us of Your goodness and of our fellowship with the saints in Christ."

God's blessings are indeed signs of His goodness, signs of His infinite love. Are we indifferent to those signs of His goodness and love? Are we so unaware of His signs that we are disconnected from Him, that we can take it or leave it? Or do we, in our daily contemplation, reflect so deeply upon those signs of His love that we are compelled, like St. Paul, to sing out such words as that hymn written way back in 1674 - amazingly enough, before even indoor plumbing and anesthesia: "Praise God from Whom all blessings flow. Praise Him all creatures here below. Praise Him above ye Heavenly hosts. Praise Father, Son, and Holy Ghost."

Prayer of Reparation

My Lord and my God, we have allowed the temptation of the devil to move our hearts toward indifference to Your divine love. We have fallen into countless times of sinful diversions from our purpose in life, which is to know, love, and serve You in this world. We are immersed in things of this world, we have devoted ourselves so greatly to treasures on earth, that we have become indifferent to the treasures we must store up in heaven. We spend so much time, effort, and money on things that moth and decay will destroy, only to discover that we still are not satisfied, we still are not happy. We turn to You Lord, in our weakness, and beg Your forgiveness for our indifference to the treasures of heaven, the greatest treasure being Your love. We love You, Lord, and we beg for the wisdom and strength to love You more. We know, Lord, if You will it, it will be done. Trusting in You, we offer our prayer to You who live and reign forever and ever. Amen.

Prayer of Exorcism

Lord God of heaven and earth, in Your power and goodness, You created all things. You set a path for us to walk on and a way to an eternal relationship. By the strength of Your arm and Word of Your mouth, cast from Your Holy Church every fearful deceit of the devil. Drive from us manifestations of the demonic that oppress us and beckon us to indifference. Still the lying tongue of the devil and his forces so that we may act freely and faithfully to Your will. Send Your holy angels to cast out all influence that the demonic entities in charge of indifference have planted in Your Church. Free us, our families, our parish, our diocese, and our country from all trickery and deceit perpetrated by the devil and his hellish legions. Trusting in Your goodness Lord, we know if You will it, it will be done, in unity with Your Son and the Holy Spirit, one God, forever and ever. Amen.

🔔 DAY 21 CHECKLIST 🔔

___ Prayer for Freedom from the Devil - pg. 255

___ Daily reflection and prayers

___ Litany of the day – pg. 256

___ Pray a Rosary (intention: exorcism of indifference) – pg.275

___ Divine Mercy Chaplet (in reparation for: sin due to indifference) – pg. 279

___ Spiritual or corporal work of mercy (see pg. 254)

___ Fast/abstain (according to level)

___ Exercise (according to level/ability)

___ Refrain from conventional media (only 1 hr. of social)

___ Examination of conscience (confession 1x this week)

Day 22
Freedom from NARCISSISM
By FR. WILLIAM PECKMAN

In Greek mythology, we find the rather tragic figure of Narcissus. As the story goes, he is an extraordinary young man in every possible way, but he is aloof and rather full of himself. Anyone who falls in love with him pays a steep price because he will not love them back. Eventually, while hunting, Narcissus stoops down to the water to get a drink. He sees his own reflection and falls madly in love with it. He reaches out to grab the reflection and drowns, suffering the abysmal fate others who tried to love him did. In psychology, narcissism is described as "selfishness, involving a sense of entitlement, a lack of empathy, and a need for admiration, as characterizing a personality type." My brothers and sisters, does this word not describe our society "to a T"?

Narcissism arises out of several converging storms: First, the self-centeredness of the individual as almighty. Reality and morality are subjectivistic and only are there to confirm the feelings of the narcissist. Second, with no empathy, the means justify the ends for the narcissist. The narcissist simply makes pronouncements without care as to how it affects others and only cares about how he or she is affected. Third, while the narcissist is free to judge and condemn the actions and words of others AND presume the absolute worst in other people's motivations, he or she will see any judgment and condemnation of their actions as defamation of character, to which they will respond with great vengeance. Fourth, the sense of absolute entitlement endemic of narcissism, stretches to the insane. Every word and action must be to the benefit of that narcissist. No demand is too unreasonable and any failure to provide is seen as a personal attack.

Certainly, within our society, we see narcissism run amuck. Social media has laced this stick of dynamite. We now are seeing a wholesale rejection of any objective truth; consequently, there cannot be a God who judges. The new mantra of society is, "It is okay to terrorize anyone we want, as long as we feel justified in our actions." According to this logic, we should be able to despoil whoever we want if our feelings tell us it's okay. It has even gotten to the point where some are demanding the acceptance of pedophilia as a mere sexual orientation, using the familiar path of others who want universal acceptance of their choices. For our narcissistic society, all things must be remade in the narcissist's image: Entertainment, sports, law, and morality must be adjusted so that the narcissist's predilections are approved at worst and ignored at best.

Even within our Church we see narcissism in several ways. We have seen it in how Mass went from a transcendent focus to a place where the transcendent is ignored. This is not anything asked for by Vatican II or present in the *General Instruction of the Roman Missal.* We see it in the constant push to revise the sexual moral teachings of the Church to be as accommodating and permissive as society, in everything from homosexuality to artificial birth control to transgenderism, and so on. The Church just becomes another place where the mirror of narcissism can be held and only able to see its world visage. So much of the financial and sexual scandal, ensuing cover-up, and regular abuse of power finds its roots in a narcissism that allows the preying on of the flock to satiate one's needs. The reach of narcissism in our society and Church is wide.

The antidote to narcissism is the very essence of God: love. Specifically, divine love (agape) is what is needed. In agape, we completely empty ourselves for the good of others. We allow ourselves, as St. Paul says, to be poured

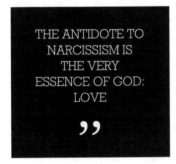

out as a libation. Love forces us to look beyond ourselves and weigh how our actions and words affect our relationships with God and each other. Love leads us to humility, a frank honesty which allows us to avoid demanding that the world convert to suit us, but instead enables us to convert to suit Christ. Because love is a theological virtue, it needs that constant relationship with God to thrive. It is no wonder that the more narcissism has grown in our society, the shorter our confession lines have become and the less we see of people at Mass. We need that sacramental presence in our lives to bolster our immunity to the constant virus-like ferocity of narcissism.

For if we love as God loves, the abuse of our neighbor is no longer justifiable. If we love as God loves, our own wants no longer become our focus. If we love as God loves, we can no longer justify our harm and sin inflicted on others. I am asking you dear reader to have what I call a "Darth Vader moment." I am referring to the scene in *Return of the Jedi* where the emperor is killing Luke for his unwillingness to convert to the dark side. In that scene, Darth Vader keeps looking at the begging face of his son and the evil cackling face of the emperor ... he is making a choice. He can either go with the status quo and allow his son to die, or lose everything, including his life, and kill the emperor (or so we thought). I am asking you to look at the Cross of Christ and then look at the fury we see in the media day after day. Choose between the great love displayed on the Cross and the insatiable fury of narcissism. We can't have both. Choose wisely, for the Cross of Christ is the path to heaven and the fury of narcissism is the superhighway to hell.

Prayer of Reparation

My Lord and my God, we have allowed the temptation of the devil to move our hearts to not see fulfillment in Your goodness. We have stilled our tongues in the face of evil. We have been too self-involved to notice the damage our sins have wreaked on our neighbor and broken faith with You. We have expected You to be pleased with our duplicitous and selfish hearts. We have, at times, been a source of scandal for those searching through our sinfulness and rebellion to You. In our fear, we have allowed the ancient foe to advance. We turn to You Lord, in our sorrow and guilt, and beg Your forgiveness for our narcissism and lack of sorrow. We beg for the grace of Your goodness to build up within us what You sought to build up in Your apostles in that tempest-tossed boat. We know, Lord, if You will it, it will be done. Trusting in You, we offer our prayer to You who live and reign forever. Amen.

Prayer of Exorcism

Lord God of heaven and earth, in Your power and goodness, You created all things. You set a path for us to walk on and a way to an eternal relationship. By the strength of Your arm and Word of Your mouth, cast from Your Holy Church every fearful deceit of the devil. Drive from us manifestations of the demonic that oppress us and beckon us to narcissism and entitlement. Still the lying tongue of the devil and his forces so that we may act freely and faithfully to Your will. Send Your holy angels to cast out all influence that the demonic entities in charge of narcissism have planted in Your Church. Free us, our families, our parish, our diocese, and our country from all trickery and deceit perpetrated by the devil and his hellish legions. Trusting in Your goodness Lord, we know if You will it, it will be done, in unity with Your Son and the Holy Spirit, one God, forever and ever. Amen.

⌂ DAY 22 CHECKLIST ⌂

___ Prayer for Freedom from the Devil - pg. 255

___ Daily reflection and prayers

___ Litany of the day – pg. 256

___ Pray a Rosary (intention: exorcism of narcissism) – pg.275

___ Divine Mercy Chaplet (in reparation for: sin due to narcissism) – pg. 279

___ Spiritual or corporal work of mercy (see pg. 254)

___ Fast/abstain (according to level)

___ Exercise (according to level/ability)

___ Refrain from conventional media (only 1 hr. of social)

___ Examination of conscience (confession 1x this week)

Day 23
Freedom from IDOLATRY
By FR. RICHARD HEILMAN

Reports surfaced that there was no cell phone activity in a high-security portion of the Wuhan Institute of Virology from October 7 through October 24, 2019, indicating that there may have been a "hazardous event" on or about October 6. On the very same day (October 6), Sr. Agnes Sasagawa of Akita received a private message ... the first since 1973 (year of infamous Roe v. Wade decision). The message was not unlike the warning Jonah received for Nineveh, in that it called for repentance: "Put on ashes and pray a repentant rosary every day."

It's more than interesting that Our Lady of Fatima appeared with her warning from May to October in 1917, urging the world to pray the rosary, repent, turn from its wicked ways, and return to the Lord, or there would be consequences. This warning came just before the 1918 plague (the Spanish Flu) broke out and claimed 50 million lives. Until now, this was the last plague in which churches were closed.

A consistent theme in the Bible is that when the people distance themselves from God and His will, which always leads to idolatry, God repeatedly allows a punishment, which is usually a plague.

Our Lady of Fatima pointed to the errors of Russia: "Russia will spread its errors throughout the world, raising up wars and persecutions against the Church." It was in

May of 1917 (just as Our Lady first appeared to the children in Fatima) that the Russian Revolution broke out, leading the way to communism. Communism is a reductively atheistic materialist worldview which aims at undermining anything Christian in society. At its essence, communism is an idolatry of man over God, and its atheistic materialist worldview has spread across the planet like a virus.

What about our time? On March 24, 2020, as we were entering the height of the COVID-19 plague's worst devastation, Bishop Strickland of Tyler, Texas, tweeted the following: "People of the world, fall to your knees. Fall to your knees to beg forgiveness of your sins. Stop worshiping yourself, stop worshiping creation, stop worshiping your desires, fall to your knees and worship God, Father, Son, and Holy Spirit. Repent!" Bishop Strickland was among many, including myself, who recognized the biblical and historic connection between idolatry and plagues.

According to paragraph 2113 of the *Catechism of the Catholic Church*, "Idolatry not only refers to false pagan worship. It remains a constant temptation to faith. Idolatry consists in divinizing what is not God. Man commits idolatry whenever he honors and reveres a creature in place of God, whether this be gods or demons (for example, Satanism), power, pleasure, race, ancestors, the state, money, etc." What do we revere ahead of God?

So many times, I have pointed to the Pew Research study from August 5, 2019, which revealed that nearly 70%

of professed Catholics don't believe in the Real Presence. 70%!!! I recall Bishop Robert Barron being shaken by this, but very few others. Personally, I believed this was a "make or break" moment in which the Church needed to act decisively, or else.

But no, instead, the talk of communion for those in mortal sin, ending celibacy for priests, women as deacons, sodomy no longer being a sin, nature worship, etc. only accelerated in the weeks and months that followed (leading up to October 2019). It became so escalated during this time, that there was even an apparent movement to "normalize" pagan idols being brought into our churches. It was as if you could hear God say, "ENOUGH!"

Okay, so what do we do? My thoughts go to Nineveh and Jonah's warning given to them. What did they do? They repented and even put on sackcloth as an outward sign of their humility before God. Most importantly, and this is repeated throughout the Bible, they put down their idols and made God the highest priority in their lives.

Now is the time for us to be honest with ourselves and ask, "What am I making a priority ahead of God in my life? What are my idols?" We must ramp up our prayer and fasting, particularly for the bishops and priests in our Church to become more and more courageous in their stand against the forces in the

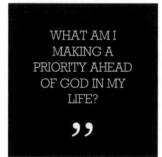

WHAT AM I MAKING A PRIORITY AHEAD OF GOD IN MY LIFE?

world who oppose God and His will. The laity must be courageous too!

Satan and his narcissistic useful idiots are emboldened, maybe as never before. Why? Because we are too busy with our idols to stand up for God and His will. The hope is that the horror of this plague and the shock of unbridled evil from sea to shining sea will bring us to our knees, as a country, as we call out to God seeking His love and His mercy!

"If my people, who are called by my name, will humble themselves and pray and seek my face and turn from their wicked ways, then I will hear from heaven, and I will forgive their sin and will heal their land" (2 Chronicles 7:14).

We love You, Lord! We are so sorry, Lord! Heal our land, Lord!

Prayer of Reparation

My Lord and my God, we have allowed the temptation of the devil to move our hearts to not see fulfillment in Your goodness. We have stilled our tongues in the face of evil. We have been too self-involved to notice the damage our sins have wreaked on our neighbor and broken faith with You. We have expected You to be pleased with our duplicitous and selfish hearts. We have, at times, been a source of scandal for those searching through our sinfulness and rebellion to You. In our fear, we have allowed the ancient foe to advance. We turn to You Lord, in our sorrow and guilt, and beg Your forgiveness for our idolatry and lack of sorrow. We beg for the grace of Your goodness to build up within us what You sought to build up in Your apostles in that tempest-tossed boat. We know, Lord, if You will it, it will be done. Trusting in You, we offer our prayer to You who live and reign forever. Amen.

Prayer of Exorcism

Lord God of heaven and earth, in Your power and goodness, You created all things. You set a path for us to walk on and a way to an eternal relationship. By the strength of Your arm and Word of Your mouth, cast from Your Holy Church every fearful deceit of the devil. Drive from us manifestations of the demonic that oppress us and beckon us to idolatry and worldliness. Still the lying tongue of the devil and his forces so that we may act freely and faithfully to Your will. Send Your holy angels to cast out all influence that the demonic entities in charge of idolatry have planted in Your Church. Free us, our families, our parish, our diocese, and our country from all trickery and deceit perpetrated by the devil and his hellish legions. Trusting in Your goodness Lord, we know if You will it, it will be done, in unity with Your Son and the Holy Spirit, one God, forever and ever. Amen.

⏶ DAY 23 CHECKLIST ⏶

___ Prayer for Freedom from the Devil - pg. 255

___ Daily reflection and prayers

___ Litany of the day – pg. 256

___ Pray a Rosary (intention: exorcism of idolatry) – pg.275

___ Divine Mercy Chaplet (in reparation for: sin due to idolatry) – pg. 279

___ Spiritual or corporal work of mercy (see pg. 254)

___ Fast/abstain (according to level)

___ Exercise (according to level/ability)

___ Refrain from conventional media (only 1 hr. of social)

___ Examination of conscience (confession 1x this week)

Day 24
Freedom from CONSUMERISM
By FR. JAMES ALTMAN

Dear family, if there was one word that might underlie the modern day "fall of mankind" it very well could be consumerism. We've heard it said that we spend a lot of money we do not have on a lot of things we do not need – especially around Christmas. Surely we all are horrified by the annual satanic feast known as "Black Friday," the day after Thanksgiving, when we reveal just how little thanks we have. We go from being "so thankful" for all the stuff we own, to rushing out in the wee hours of the morning to stand in line (in all kinds of weather), to be one of the first people through the door to buy a bunch more stuff. Dear family, the only Black Friday a good Catholic knows is Good Friday, for we know that on that blackest day in human history, when it seemed Lucifer had his victory, Easter Sunday was coming. How much less would we consume on the satanic holiday of Black Friday if our eyes were focused on The Resurrection of Jesus the Lord on Easter Sunday?

IT IS A BEHAVIOR THAT COMPENSATES FOR THE HOLE WITHIN US...

"

Consumerism is a compensating behavior. It is a behavior that compensates for the hole within us, the hurts and wounds we have accumulated, the woundedness and brokenness from which we all suffer. When we have a headache we have our go-to drug of choice, Excedrin, Tylenol or whatever. When we are hurting in our hearts and souls, we have our go-to compensating behavior. Our compensating behaviors are as addictive as any drug or any other vice into which we fall. We use it to compensate for our suffering. Such is consumerism. As with any addiction or vice, it only is a temporary anesthetic, something that relieves the suffering only temporarily. Ultimately, it is a suffering that only can be healed and filled by Divine Love.

Why is it that humanity is so susceptible to falling into compensating behaviors like consumerism, and so quick to forsake the Divine Healer? Why is it that we think more stuff will ever be enough?

It is well understood that affluence is a faith-killer. When we have all we need (indeed way more than we need) and when we can rely upon ourselves to obtain or accumulate what we think we want, we tend to forsake God. The day we think we do not have to rely upon God is the day we begin to drift away, very quickly immersing ourselves in immediate gratification through our own devices. Most certainly, we forget Jesus' admonition:

"If God so clothes the grass of the field, which grows today and is thrown into the oven tomorrow, will he not much more provide for you, O you of little faith? So do not worry and say, 'What are we to eat?' or 'What are we to drink?' or 'What are we to wear?' All these things the pagans seek. Your heavenly Father knows that you need them all. But seek first the kingdom [of God] and his righteousness, and all these things will be given you besides" (Matthew 6:30-33).

Anecdotally, Ireland once was an extremely poor country yet, at the same time, a rock-bed of Catholicism. Enter the economic boom of the 1990s-early 2000's. It was a time of such spectacular economic growth in Ireland that it had its own nickname: Celtic Tiger. Faith fell away. Interestingly, Ireland still has about the lowest divorce rate in the Western world, less than a third of the United States. However, recently Ireland legalized abortion and same-sex marriage and – not in small part due to the horrific failure amongst bishops and the abuse scandal – faith has decreased significantly. Similarly, from the first time I went on pilgrimage to the Sanctuary of Divine Mercy in Poland in 2001, to the last time in 2017, there not only has been a very visible increase in affluence but, sadly, an increase of the seeds of immorality being sown in the public square (Beware of the young woman holding an umbrella in the broad daylight).

Here's the thing about consumerism. We already contemplated the Life Lesson of Adam and Eve – how nothing ever is enough. Far worse than that, consumerism cannot heal. Only the Divine Healer can heal the wounds within us. Only Divine Mercy can heal.

Dear family, we can build ourselves a bigger house, surround ourselves with more stuff in the house, get a bigger SUV to go get more stuff for the house – but nothing compares to being in a genuine Catholic Church, God's house, where His Son is present in the Real

Presence. Nothing we can buy, nothing we can accumulate, absolutely nothing, will heal our hearts and minds and souls like being in the presence of the Real Presence. That being the case, why is it that we spend a lot more time at work, working so hard to earn some money, to pay the bills that arise from buying – consuming - so much stuff we don't need? All we really must do is spend a little less time consuming and a little more time with Jesus.

We used to have a Catholic devotion, a Catholic tradition, of stopping by the Church daily, even for just a few minutes. We were born and raised knowing that Jesus not only is present, but He waits for us in the Tabernacle. He thirsts for us to come and keep Him company. Do we understand that if we just spent a little bit of time in His Real Presence every day, something we do need, we would feel a lot less need to spend a lot of money to consume so much other stuff we do not need?

Prayer of Reparation

My Lord and my God, we have allowed the temptation of the devil to move our hearts toward consumerism. We have fallen into countless times of sinfully buying stuff we do not need with money we do not have. We do this all to fill the emptiness within us, to salve the wounds within us. We turn so readily to consuming things of this world, instead of detaching ourselves from things of this world and attaching ourselves to You. We spend so much time and effort and money consuming and yet we still are not happy. We turn to You Lord, in our weakness, and beg

Your forgiveness for the consumption of temporal goods that stand in the way of our devotion to You. We love You, Lord, and we beg for the wisdom and strength to love You more. We know, Lord, if You will it, it will be done. Trusting in You, we offer our prayer to You who live and reign forever and ever. Amen.

Prayer of Exorcism

Lord God of heaven and earth, in Your power and goodness, You created all things. You set a path for us to walk on and a way to an eternal relationship. By the strength of Your arm and Word of Your mouth, cast from Your Holy Church every fearful deceit of the devil. Drive from us manifestations of the demonic that oppress us and beckon us to consumerism. Still the lying tongue of the devil and his forces so that we may act freely and faithfully to Your will. Send Your holy angels to cast out all influence that the demonic entities in charge of consumerism have planted in Your Church. Free us, our families, our parish, our diocese, and our country from all trickery and deceit perpetrated by the devil and his hellish legions. Trusting in Your goodness Lord, we know if You will it, it will be done, in unity with Your Son and the Holy Spirit, one God, forever and ever. Amen.

☖ DAY 24 CHECKLIST ☖

___ Prayer for Freedom from the Devil - pg. 255

___ Daily reflection and prayers

___ Litany of the day – pg. 256

___ Pray a Rosary (intention: exorcism of consumerism) – pg.275

___ Divine Mercy Chaplet (in reparation for: sin due to consumerism) – pg. 279

___ Spiritual or corporal work of mercy (see pg. 254)

___ Fast/abstain (according to level)

___ Exercise (according to level/ability)

___ Refrain from conventional media (only 1 hr. of social)

___ Examination of conscience (confession 1x this week)

Day 25
Freedom from WRATH
By FR. WILLIAM PECKMAN

In the medieval classic, *The Divine Comedy: Inferno*, Dante places the wrathful in the 5th circle of Hell. The wrathful spend eternity forever fighting each other on the surface of the River Styx while the sullen and resentful gurgle beneath the surface of the river. These are fitting punishments for the wrathful. For the warlike wrathful (those who actively engage in harm to those who harmed them) it is fitting that they spend eternity forever inflicting the eternal cycle that revenge begets. It is appropriate as well that the embittered and resentful drown in a river of their passive-aggressiveness and resentment. In either case, wrath is unable to produce any positive in a person's life.

As a connoisseur of social media, on more than one occasion I have seen memes saying that moments of righteous indignation are okay because Jesus toppled tables of moneychangers and livestock sellers in the temple as if what we are witnessing is a divine temper tantrum. Is Jesus really indulging in a deadly sin? No. More on that in a bit.

Wrath has become quite dominant in our culture right now. Real and perceived injustices are both met with a carte blanche to seek retribution through violent means. Real perpetrators, or even innocent bystanders, are punished in a wave of violence that can only beget a backlash that perpetuates more violence. For the wrathful, any slight, real or perceived, is just grounds for vicious retribution and despoiling of reputation through gossip, detraction, and calumny. The devil himself is full of wrath. His anger with God at creating humanity, and seeing that as a slight against him and the other fallen angels, has become cause for him to wage an eternal battle with not just God but with His creation. All temptation is generated by the devil's eternal resentment and rebellion against God. The devil in his pride loves nothing more than for us to engage in his same behavior of wrath. Misery loves company.

Jesus places a premium on mercy and forgiveness in the Gospels...even from the Cross. He tells us, "But I say to you, love your enemies: do good to them that hate you: and pray for

JESUS PLACES A PREMIUM ON MERCY AND FORGIVENESS IN THE GOSPELS...

them that persecute and calumniate you: Then you will prove yourselves sons of Your heavenly Father" (Matthew 5:44-45). Similar lines are repeated in the Gospels multiple times. What then of flipping tables? We are told Jesus is full of zeal and not wrath. These things did not belong in the temple area. His expulsion of these things was not a divine hissy fit, but a sign that He came to restore what was needed and cast out what was not. He is not avenging Himself on these sellers; He is exorcising from the Temple what is foreign to it.

The antidote for wrath is, as we see above, mercy and forgiveness. There are two things to understand in this. First, to forgive means to no longer hold against (as in a loan) a person their debt/trespass/sin for future reference. It does not mean to condone or rationalize evil done to you. Mercy is to render to another person what is needed, whether they deserve it or not. In many homilies, I have referred to mercy and forgiveness as the ultimate acts of self-preservation. Wrath can ruin us on every level of our being. Mercy frees us from such a cross of iron.

It is incredibly important that we forgive. Our eternal life in heaven hinges on our ability to do so. In the Our Father we pray, "forgive us our trespasses as we forgive those who trespass against us!" In other words: "God, forgive me as I forgive others." That little prayer tucked into the Our Father can either be a blessing or an eternal curse depending upon our ability to forgive and our ability to stem wrath in our lives. After giving us the Our Father, Jesus warns us, "For if you will forgive men their offenses, your heavenly Father will forgive you also your offenses. But if you will not forgive men, neither will your Father forgive you your offenses" (Matthew 6:14-15). We entertain wrath and revenge at our own peril. We run the risk of the wicked servant in Matthew 18:23-35 who, because he was unwilling to forgive the much lesser debt of a fellow servant after he himself had a huge debt forgiven by the master, was now thrown into prison. It ends with the rather ominous "So my Father will do to you if you do not forgive your brother from your heart." Wrath can have no hold in the life of a follower of Christ.

Prayer of Reparation

My Lord and my God, we have allowed the temptation of the devil to move our hearts to wrath and vengeance against those who have harmed us. We have engaged in active revenge or in the passive-aggressiveness of gossip. We have been too self-involved to notice the damage our sins have wreaked on our neighbor and broken faith with You. We have expected You to turn a blind eye to our wrath and forgive us without condition. We have, at times, been a source of scandal for those searching through our sinfulness and rebellion to You. In our fear, we have allowed the ancient foe to advance. We turn to You Lord, in our sorrow and guilt, and beg Your forgiveness for our wrath and lack of mercy and forgiveness. We beg for the grace of Your goodness to build up within us what You sought to build up in Your apostles in that tempest-tossed boat. We know, Lord, if You will it, it will be done. Trusting in You, we offer our prayer to You who live and reign forever. Amen.

Prayer of Exorcism

Lord God of heaven and earth, in Your power and goodness, You created all things. You set a path for us to walk on and a way to an eternal relationship. By the strength of Your arm and Word of Your mouth, cast from Your Holy Church every fearful deceit of the devil. Drive from us manifestations of the demonic that oppress us and beckon us to wrath. Still the lying tongue of the devil and his forces so that we may act freely and faithfully to Your will. Send Your holy angels to cast out all influence that the demonic entities in charge of wrath have planted in Your Church. Free us, our families, our parish, our diocese, and our country from all trickery and deceit perpetrated by the devil and his hellish legions. Trusting in Your goodness Lord, we know if You will it, it will be done, in unity with Your Son and the Holy Spirit, one God, forever and ever. Amen.

🔔 DAY 25 CHECKLIST 🔔

__ Prayer for Freedom from the Devil - pg. 255

__ Daily reflection and prayers

__ Litany of the day – pg. 256

__ Pray a Rosary (intention: exorcism of wrath) – pg.275

__ Divine Mercy Chaplet (in reparation for: sin due to wrath) – pg. 279

__ Spiritual or corporal work of mercy (see pg. 254)

__ Fast/abstain (according to level)

__ Exercise (according to level/ability)

__ Refrain from conventional media (only 1 hr. of social)

__ Examination of conscience (confession 1x this week)

Day 26
Freedom from PRIDE
By FR. RICHARD HEILMAN

Pride is the "Biggie." This is the sin Satan committed in his choice to refuse to submit to God. This is the "original sin" that infected our first parents — "You will be like God" - and every generation that followed. In fact, without the waters of baptism, empowering us to stand against the original sin, along with a daily commitment to keep our "personal pride radar" up and on high alert, we can very easily slip into the intoxicating grip of pride. If we are not careful, we can find it driving just about every sin we commit. Pope St. Gregory the Great counted pride as the "mother of all sins."

Pride, in fact, is the sin that is most at work to divide

PRIDE, IN FACT, IS THE SIN THAT IS MOST AT WORK TO DIVIDE AND DESTROY OUR CULTURE

and destroy our culture. Think about this, Adam and Eve, to their ruin, believed that "freedom" was defined as the freedom from adhering to the will of God. They wanted the ability to "Just Do It," to do as they pleased and determine for themselves what was right and wrong. They believed they had "progressed" beyond God.

There's that seemingly indisputable term: "progress." Or, as its adherents refer to themselves, "progressives." By and large, this is a movement to remake whatever is determined to be archaic and no longer applicable, by the generation who has thankfully, "arrived on the scene" (sarcasm alert). They claim to have a kind of gnostic understanding of things that the "common folk" do not possess. They often make the lofty proclamation that they have "evolved." What is archaic? What have they evolved from? GOD!

In fact, God, and His adherents, are a threat to the agenda of the "evolved." In their eyes, the Dark Age's notions must be destroyed. Notions such as seeing faith as a positive influence in the culture; revering and protecting the child in the womb; supporting the bedrock of civilization – the nuclear family; seeking care, housing and assistance for those dealing with psychological disorders and addictions ... many of which are abandoned on the streets (e.g., drug addicts, homosexuals, those with gender dysphoria, etc.); banning the slavery of prostitution and child sex-trafficking; supporting a healthy economy to assist people off of government assistance and giving them the dignity of work; healing, instead of stoking, racial division; seeking quality education for our children (over kowtowing to unions who fill politicians' coffers); having a patriotic heart for our country; honoring and thanking the heroic lives of police, military, first responders, and all those who put themselves in harm's way to protect us and our freedoms.

In today's culture, if you hold these truths to be self-evident (to borrow a phrase) - notions that find their source in our faith in God - YOU are the problem! YOU are causing division. And YOU must be silenced or even assaulted. In other words, the so-called progressives have granted to themselves the right to dictate to everyone else what is right and wrong. They are the arbiters of what is considered the "new normal" of values. They have made themselves gods.

Add to this, that fitting in has become compulsive among far too many. Those who seek to preserve the best qualities of our culture, founded in God, have become targets for the "evolved." We have now found ourselves in a place where it has become socially acceptable to ridicule, shame, and even physically attack those who are not adhering to the new values. Many are even on the receiving end of this socially acceptable abuse from family members and friends.

Humility opposes pride. Not that we are called to let ourselves be a "whipping boy" to bolster others' lust for superiority. Humility is a reverence for the truth; a reverence for who we are and what we are called to be; a reverence for the reason we even exist - God. Humility opens the door to the spirit of gratitude. In our abundant gratitude for all God has done (beginning with setting us into existence) and is doing, we say "YES" to God, and a big fat "NO" to the incessant propaganda of a new normal of lies that directly oppose the will of God.

Like the heroic first Christians, we go about radiating our love for God and neighbor, while we are willing to die for the TRUTH. This was why the first Christians grew in number so rapidly. They were attractive because they were

HEROIC! Now is the time, possibly more than any other time in salvation history, for more and more souls to rise up, as the first Christians did, with that humble and heroic light of truth and love.

Prayer of Reparation

My Lord and my God, we have allowed the temptation of the devil to move our hearts to not see fulfillment in Your goodness. We have stilled our tongues in the face of evil. We have been too self-involved to notice the damage our sins have wreaked on our neighbor and broken faith with You. We have expected You to be pleased with our prideful and selfish hearts. We have, at times, been a source of scandal for those searching through our pridefulness and rebellion to You. In our fear, we have allowed the ancient foe to advance. We turn to You Lord, in our sorrow and guilt, and beg Your forgiveness for our pride and lack of sorrow. We beg for the grace of Your goodness to build up within us what You sought to build up in Your apostles in that tempest-tossed boat. We know, Lord, if You will it, it will be done. Trusting in You, we offer our prayer to You who live and reign forever. Amen.

Prayer of Exorcism

Lord God of heaven and earth, in Your power and goodness, You created all things. You set a path for us to walk on and a way to an eternal relationship. By the strength of Your arm and Word of Your mouth, cast from Your Holy Church every fearful deceit of the devil. Drive

from us manifestations of the demonic that oppress us and beckon us to pride. Still the lying tongue of the devil and his forces so that we may act freely and faithfully to Your will. Send Your holy angels to cast out all influence that the demonic entities in charge of pride have planted in Your Church. Free us, our families, our parish, our diocese, and our country from all trickery and deceit perpetrated by the devil and his hellish legions. Trusting in Your goodness Lord, we know if You will it, it will be done, in unity with Your Son and the Holy Spirit, one God, forever and ever. Amen.

⌂ DAY 26 CHECKLIST ⌂

__ Prayer for Freedom from the Devil - pg. 255
__ Daily reflection and prayers
__ Litany of the day – pg. 256
__ Pray a Rosary (intention: exorcism of pride) – pg.275
__ Divine Mercy Chaplet (in reparation for: sin due to pride) – pg. 279
__ Spiritual or corporal work of mercy (see pg. 254)
__ Fast/abstain (according to level)
__ Exercise (according to level/ability)
__ Refrain from conventional media (only 1 hr. of social)
__ Examination of conscience (confession 1x this week)

Day 27
Freedom from GLUTTONY
By FR. JAMES ALTMAN

Dear family, we all have heard of the Seven Deadly Sins, even if we cannot remember all seven on the spot. By the time you get done with the *Let Freedom Ring* training, all three of us will have written on every one, so you likely could "get" seven out of seven. In a random poll, however, while most would remember pride, greed, and lust, and probably most would remember gluttony – as for sloth, wrath, and envy, not so much. As a confessor, it must be said that most people do not seem to do an adequate and sufficient examination of conscience; they don't often discuss those times when they have fallen into these deadly sins. When they are confessed, sometimes it's pride, many, many times it's lust, and occasionally it's envy and gluttony. Again, as to the others, not so much. Maybe the deadliest part of any of these is that we do not pay enough attention to them, and that may be because we

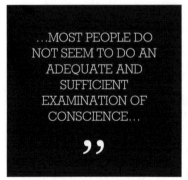

...MOST PEOPLE DO NOT SEEM TO DO AN ADEQUATE AND SUFFICIENT EXAMINATION OF CONSCIENCE...

99

have not taken the time to meditate upon the fullness of the sin.

Gluttony usually is defined in relation to food, but really could be defined as the overindulgence and overconsumption of anything to the point of waste. The "food" aspect is derived from the Latin *gluttire*, meaning to gulp down or swallow.

St. Thomas Aquinas took a more expansive view of gluttony, arguing that it could also include an obsessive anticipation of meals. Aquinas prepared a list of five ways to commit gluttony, one of which was eating too much. Another "ardenter" – was eating too eagerly. Of these, ardenter was often considered the most serious, since it is extreme attachment to the pleasure of mere eating (I'm not sure if my attachment to Flaming Hot Cheetos falls into this category, but when I use it as a breakfast comfort food, I'm probably skating on thin ice!) Aquinas said ardenter can make the committer eat impulsively; absolutely and without qualification live merely to eat and drink; lose attachment to health-related, social, intellectual, and spiritual pleasures; and lose proper judgement. (Pretty sure I'm not there yet, on those Flaming Hot Cheetos.)

The great Fr. John Hardon's *Modern Catholic Dictionary* defines gluttony thusly: "Inordinate desire for the pleasure connected with food or drink. This desire may become sinful in various ways: by eating or drinking far more than a person needs to maintain bodily strength; by glutting one's taste for certain kinds of food with known detriment to health; by indulging the appetite for exquisite food or drink, especially when these are beyond one's ability to afford a luxurious diet; by eating or drinking too avidly, i.e., ravenously; by consuming alcoholic beverages to the point of losing full control of one's reasoning powers.

Intoxication that ends in complete loss of reason is a mortal sin ...."

Donald Attwater's *A Catholic Dictionary* also points out that this rising to the level of mortal sin occurs when food consumption is excessive to the point of causing health issues, or drinking is excessive to the point of intoxication.

The point of all this – which may border on TMI (too much information) – is that if we do not know what we are talking about, how will we ever know if we are, as mentioned, possibly skating on that thin ice?

The bottom line – gluttony easily can be understood as eating and drinking too much. It is fair to say that Americans fall much more into the category of Rich Man Dives: "There was a rich man who dressed in purple garments and fine linen and dined sumptuously each day" (Luke 16:19), than we fall into the category of Poor Man Lazarus: "And lying at [Dives'] door was a poor man named Lazarus, covered with sores, who would gladly have eaten his fill of the scraps that fell from the rich man's table. Dogs even used to come and lick his sores" (Luke 16:20-21). And that will be a problem one day, because we all know where Dives ended up — yes, the eternal tormenting fires of hell! How much better to aspire to the example of St. Teresa of Calcutta who served the poorest of the poor, who served all the "Poor Man Lazaruses" of Calcutta.

We are well off in America. In fact, it has been said that the poorest Americans are richer than the richest third-world-citizens. Are we so gluttonous, has gluttony become so much a part of our day-to-day, that we do not even recognize it for what it is? Are we just like Dives? He seemed clueless, didn't he? And yet, remember in Jesus' parable, it was not like Dives did not know Poor Man Lazarus. In the reality to which Jesus spoke, Dives practically would have had to trip over Lazarus every time he went in and out of the front gate. We actually know that Dives knew exactly who Lazarus was, because Dives called him by name when Dives appealed to Abraham: "Father Abraham, have pity on me. Send Lazarus to dip the tip of his finger in water and cool my tongue, for I am suffering torment in these flames" (Luke 16:24).

Dear family, let us take time to realize just how much we have, how much we consume (especially food and alcohol), and then ponder whether we genuinely have fasted from either. Have we freed up and offered some of our wealth for the benefit of the Lazaruses who might be sitting outside our own front gate?

Prayer of Reparation

My Lord and my God, we have allowed the temptation of the devil to move our hearts toward gluttony. Countless times we have sat down to a feast, unconcerned about our own health and welfare, and even more condemnably, unconcerned about those who would long to eat the scraps from our tables. We are so immersed in the pleasures of eating and drinking, that we hardly recognize when we eat or drink to excess. We think this excess really is no big deal. We so often do not attribute sin to this excess and fail to confess the very thing which the bathroom scales and the hangovers make so evident. We spend so much time and effort and money on feasting, and so little time and effort on fasting, even though we know, for we have been told, some things only may be attained through prayer and fasting. We turn to You Lord, in our weakness, and beg Your forgiveness for our gluttony – for our selfish and excessive self-indulgence in food and drink. We love You, Lord, and we beg for the wisdom and strength to love You more. We know Lord, if You will it, it will be done. Trusting in You, we offer our prayer to You who live and reign forever and ever. Amen.

Prayer of Exorcism

Lord God of heaven and earth, in Your power and goodness, You created all things. You set a path for us to walk on and a way to an eternal relationship. By the strength of Your arm and Word of Your mouth, cast from Your Holy Church every fearful deceit of the devil. Drive from us manifestations of the demonic that oppress us and beckon us to gluttony. Still the lying tongue of the devil and his forces so that we may act freely and faithfully to Your will. Send Your holy angels to cast out all influence that the demonic entities in charge of gluttony have planted in Your Church. Free us, our families, our parish, our diocese, and our country from all trickery and deceit perpetrated by the devil and his hellish legions. Trusting in Your goodness Lord, we know if You will it, it will be done, in unity with Your Son and the Holy Spirit, one God, forever and ever. Amen.

♘ DAY 27 CHECKLIST ♘

___ Prayer for Freedom from the Devil - pg. 255

___ Daily reflection and prayers

___ Litany of the day – pg. 256

___ Pray a Rosary (intention: exorcism of gluttony) – pg.275

___ Divine Mercy Chaplet (in reparation for: sin due to gluttony) – pg. 279

___ Spiritual or corporal work of mercy (see pg. 254)

___ Fast/abstain (according to level)

___ Exercise (according to level/ability)

___ Refrain from conventional media (only 1 hr. of social)

___ Examination of conscience (confession 1x this week)

Day 28
Freedom from RACISM
By FR. WILLIAM PECKMAN

As dominant a topic as racism is today, the word is only 140 years old in usage. I have been reading the book *The Guarded Gate* by Daniel Okrent. He traces how both nativism and eugenics in 19th Century America and Northern Europe led to the closing of the U.S.A.'s doors to immigrants in the 1920's from groups deemed to be lesser races. Race didn't exclusively refer to the color of one's skin as it does today. Races were divided by religion and nationality as well. The likes of Sen. Henry Cabot Lodge would have been indignant at the idea that a WASP (White Anglo-Saxon Protestant) such as himself, would have been put in the same race as Poles, Russians, Slavs, Italians, Spaniards, Irish Catholics, Catholics, or Jews. This type of racism found its most deadly form in the Third Reich in Nazi Germany. Hitler, being a northern European, also sent Slavs, Poles, Roma (aka Gypsies), Russians, Catholics (especially clergy and seminarians), as well as Jews to the concentration/death camps.

The notion of racism these days fully arises out of eugenics. For those who do not know what eugenics is, it is a belief that humanity can become a super race by eliminating what are considered lesser strains, or human "weeds". English scientist Thomas Galton began this controversial study based on the extension of the work of his cousin, Charles Darwin. The Nativist movement in the

U.S. and the U.K. picked up on this and found a particular champion in America with Planned Parenthood founder, Margaret Sanger. It was she who designated the entirety of those with black skin to be among the lesser of humanity, taking a view of them akin to the slave traders and owners who 50 years prior sought to keep them enslaved.

Racism is another way that Satan sets us against each other. It is another potent dividing line. Although he

RACISM IS ANOTHER WAY THAT SATAN SETS US AGAINST EACH OTHER

doesn't address race in his epistles (mainly because the concept is non-existent), St. Paul writes many times how these manmade divisions are inappropriate to the Body of Christ. He says that in Christ, there is no male or female, Jew or Greek, slave or freeman (Galatians 3:28). It takes little effort to imagine he would extend this to the idea that in Christ there are no races, but that all in Christ are one despite manmade differentiations and the superior/inferior delegations we put to them.

Racism is tearing apart our country right now. It is a tool used by people with hopes of tearing down this country and reconstituting it as a communist or socialist nation. Both ideologies require struggles between an oppressed class and oppressor class to justify upending the system. They have simply borrowed the categories from other totalitarian groups, such as the Nazi's, and tweaked them to suit the new narrative. They can do this because we have 150 or so years of fomenting the idea of racism.

There have been incidents of racism within the Church. When one looks at the story of Fr. Augustine Tolton, declared venerable by the Church, we see a black man and former slave who was called by God to the priesthood yet could not find an American seminary to take him. I believe that racism, in a soft form, has largely gutted inner city parishes where the natives refused or failed in evangelizing the new people moving in because they didn't look like them. To be honest, I have heard more than a few times, vile racial slurs from those who claim to be good Catholics. Such things, as St. Paul would remind us, are wholly unacceptable behaviors for a follower of Jesus and have no place within the Body of Christ.

It is our society that likes dividing the population into separate corporate bodies to pit them against each other. Certainly, more nefarious political systems need and thrive upon such divisions. Within the Body of Christ, this is wholly evil. One of the marks of the Church is 'One' — that is, that we are one in Christ. That oneness is not subservient to worldly divisions and political jostling. Consider that the Catholic Church has over 1.4 billion members. Those 1.4 billion come from every conceivable culture, language, and skin color, yet we are called to be one. That oneness starts here and stretches to eternity.

What is needed is wisdom, that gift of the Holy Spirit that enables us to see one another as Christ sees us. First and foremost, He sees each of us as needing God's love and grace. He sees each of us as redeemable and worth the price of the Cross. We need to see each other in such a light. When someone searching comes upon us, they should not see us looking like the world, but they should see us in stark contrast to the world. We don't seek to divide what is called to be one. Over the years, I have thought it asinine to make judgements about the character of a person based on how much melanin happens to be in their skin. Wisdom leads us to truth. Truth leads us to love. God is love. Let us pray for the courage to look at the agent provocateurs who use race (and any other category they can find) to pit us against each other, and instead choose to love each other as God loves us.

Prayer of Reparation

My Lord and my God, we have allowed the temptation of the devil to move our hearts to not see fulfillment in Your goodness. We have stilled our tongues in the face of evil. We have allowed false divisions to wreak destruction on our society and Church. We have expected You to be pleased with our divisiveness. We have, at times, been a source of scandal for those searching through our sinfulness and rebellion to You. In our fear, we have allowed the ancient foe to advance. We turn to You Lord, in our sorrow and guilt, and beg Your forgiveness for our racism. We beg for the grace of Your goodness to build up within us what You sought to build up in Your apostles in that tempest-tossed boat. We know Lord, if You will it, it will be done. Trusting in You, we offer our prayer to You who live and reign forever and ever. Amen.

Prayer of Exorcism

Lord God of heaven and earth, in Your power and goodness, You created all things. You set a path for us to walk on and a way to an eternal relationship. By the strength of Your arm and Word of Your mouth, cast from Your Holy Church every fearful deceit of the devil. Drive from us manifestations of the demonic that oppress us and beckon us to racism and entitlement. Still the lying tongue of the devil and his forces so that we may act freely and faithfully to Your will. Send Your holy angels to cast out all influence that the demonic entities in charge of racism have planted in Your Church. Free us, our families, our parish, our diocese, and our country from all trickery and deceit perpetrated by the devil and his hellish legions. Trusting in Your goodness Lord, we know if You will it, it will be done, in unity with Your Son and the Holy Spirit, One God forever and ever. Amen.

☖ DAY 28 CHECKLIST ☖

___ Prayer for Freedom from the Devil - pg. 255

___ Daily reflection and prayers

___ Litany of the day – pg. 256

___ Pray a Rosary (intention: exorcism of racism) –
pg.275

___ Divine Mercy Chaplet (in reparation for: sin due to
racism) – pg. 279

___ Spiritual or corporal work of mercy (see pg. 254)

___ Fast/abstain (according to level)

___ Exercise (according to level/ability)

___ Refrain from conventional media (only 1 hr. of social)

___ Examination of conscience (confession 1x this week)

Day 29
Freedom from ACEDIA
By FR. RICHARD HEILMAN

Recently, I wrote a reflection on pride. I said, "Pride is the Biggie," because it's "the sin that is most at work to divide and destroy our culture." Although I believe that to be true, I would say the most dominant sin that characterizes our culture today is acedia. Acedia has been referred to as the "noonday devil."

"Acedia" originates from the Greek, *akèdia*, meaning "lack of care." It's a kind of indifference or a "lack of spiritual energy," which is a phrase from the book by Jean-Charles Nault, O.S.B., *The Noonday devil: Acedia, the Unnamed Evil of Our Times*. Nault, the abbot of the Benedictine Abbey of Saint-Wandrille in France, is one of the world's experts on acedia. I recall the acclaim this book had in 2015, and I ordered it right away. I highly recommend it.

Nault references how it came to be called, "the noonday devil." In the writings of Evagrius of Pontus (345-399, one of the Desert Fathers), he explained that acedia manifests itself as a temptation for the monk to depart his cell. This temptation is often worst around midday, hence the "noonday devil."

The reasons for abandoning his cell could all be reasonable or even noble: He may want to work on his health, or he is just seeking a change of scenery, or maybe he wants to visit family, or he believes he could help more people outside his cell. Therefore, acedia doesn't necessarily always have to do with laziness. It could be manifested in activism.

Acedia can often be associated with "spiritual instability," a kind of restlessness. So, the soul may find itself horrified by its commitments, even abhor the spiritual life. The soul finds itself stuck in a kind of spiritual malaise which prevents it from advancing in the spiritual life.

St. Thomas Aquinas said of acedia that it is a "sadness about spiritual good." It's a sadness of even the ultimate good of union with God. How can that be? St. Thomas says that man can become sad at the prospect of union with God because it requires him to give up goods to which he is attached.

Once someone detaches from their call to advance in the spiritual life, they can become satisfied with what St. Thomas calls a mere "animal beatitude." In other words, we demote ourselves to mere animals, aimlessly feeding the flesh with all its lust and wants. Once this fails, and it usually does, we are left to fall into a nihilism, or even a hatred of being.

...WE DEMOTE OURSELVES TO MERE ANIMALS, AIMLESSLY FEEDING THE FLESH WITH ALL ITS LUST AND WANTS

For a soul adrift in acedia, and therefore unstable with loss of meaning and purpose in life, he is left to vacillate between reducing himself to just another animal species, or worse, a blight on an otherwise perfect natural world. Is this sounding familiar yet? It should be; it is pervasive thought in a world becoming more and more disconnected from God.

How did we get here, and how do we get out of this epidemic of acedia in our culture, and even in our Church? I continue to believe we Catholics deserve much of the blame. Why? This is where I point to a previous reflection I gave on lukewarmness. Recall it was Pope St. Pius V who went so far as to say, "All the evil in the world is due to lukewarm Catholics."

If we are the one true Church founded by Jesus Christ - and we are - then we were called to lift the world out of the emptiness of acedia that leads to believing we are mere animals. Yet, for more than 50 years, we have been peddling a weak and watered-down religion; a religion that denies the power of God; a religion of "activism" that seems to abhor the call to advance in the spiritual life. It almost seems like the proponents of this modern-day Catholic religion were (and are), themselves, plagued with acedia. Some even militate against a restoration of sacred beauty and sacred worship. "It's too much," they proclaim. "People won't like our Church if we promote all the 'sacred stuff.'" In essence, they are saying, "We need to be a 'Church of Acedia' in order to reach those caught in acedia." And so, the acedia is left to spread like a virus.

In Paul's letter to Timothy, he warned about just such a time as ours: "But mark this: There will be terrible times in the last days. People will be lovers of themselves, lovers of money, boastful, proud, abusive, disobedient to their parents, ungrateful, unholy, without love, unforgiving, slanderous, without self-control, brutal, not lovers of the good, treacherous, rash, conceited, lovers of pleasure rather than lovers of God— having a form of godliness but denying its power. Have nothing to do with such people" (2 Timothy 3:1-5).

Thank God, many are talking about the need for us to repent. But repent from what? We must repent from creating a Church that has the "form of godliness but denies its power." This renewed faith and trust in the power of God, and worshiping as though we actually believe in it, is the antidote for our global pandemic: acedia.

Prayer of Reparation

My Lord and my God, we have allowed the temptation of the devil to move our hearts toward fearfully allowing the spread of acedia throughout our nation and the Catholic Church. We have fallen into this widespread acedia when we have not lived up to the call of our baptism to, day-by-day, deepen our love and faith in You. We have been too easily swayed by the poor example of the Catholic acedia, in churches everywhere, and have not encouraged a deeper sense of supernatural faith. In our weakness, we have allowed the ancient foe to advance. We turn to You Lord, in our sorrow and guilt, and beg Your forgiveness for any of our own acedia or our lack of resolve to lift souls out of this spiritual malaise. We beg for the grace of Your goodness to build up within us the strength and endurance to be this visible light of fervent faith in You. We know Lord, if You will it, it will be done. Trusting in You, we offer our prayer to You who live and reign forever and ever. Amen.

Prayer of Exorcism

Lord God of heaven and earth, in Your power and goodness, You created all things. You set a path for us to walk on and a way to an eternal relationship. By the strength of Your arm and Word of Your mouth, cast from Your Holy Church every fearful deceit of the devil. Drive from us manifestations of the demonic that oppress us and beckon us to acedia. Still the lying tongue of the devil and his forces so that we may act freely and faithfully to do Your will. Send Your holy angels to cast out all influence that the demonic entities in charge of acedia have planted in Your Church. Free us, our families, our parish, our diocese, and our country from all trickery and deceit perpetrated by the devil and his hellish legions. Trusting in Your goodness Lord, we know if You will it, it will be done, in unity with Your Son and the Holy Spirit, One God forever and ever. Amen.

♤ DAY 29 CHECKLIST ♤

___ Prayer for Freedom from the Devil - pg. 255

___ Daily reflection and prayers

___ Litany of the day – pg. 256

___ Pray a Rosary (intention: exorcism of acedia) –
pg.275

___ Divine Mercy Chaplet (in reparation for: sin due to
acedia) – pg. 279

___ Spiritual or corporal work of mercy (see pg. 254)

___ Fast/abstain (according to level)

___ Exercise (according to level/ability)

___ Refrain from conventional media (only 1 hr. of social)

___ Examination of conscience (confession 1x this week)

Day 30
Freedom from SECULARISM
By FR. JAMES ALTMAN

Dear family, I'm not quite sure whether it was Fr. Heilman or Fr. Peckman who "assigned" the topics – but I am sure it was guided by the Holy Spirit! Consequently, I was blessed to have secularism among my topics. If you ever want to "push my buttons," just bring it up! So we are clear on what button is getting pushed, the term "secularism" was first used by the British writer George Holyoake in 1851. He invented the term secularism to describe his views of promoting a social order separate from religion – like that ever would be a good idea - without actively dismissing or criticizing religious belief.

Obviously, given its date of creation, secularism, in word and in deed, was not a principle stated in the Constitution. For the record, what the Constitution does state in the Establishment Clause is, "Congress shall make no law respecting an establishment of religion, or prohibiting the free exercise thereof." The unanimous understanding of this clause had to do solely with preventing the national government from creating – like Henry VIII – a religion enforceable through government police power. This truth is confirmed by the prohibition against prohibiting "the free exercise thereof." Understand, dear family, that this applied only to the federal government, while states had the right to establish a particular religion. Few people know and understand that the Establishment Clause of the First Amendment, which clearly prohibits the creation of a national church, did not eliminate established churches in those states where they still existed. Indeed, it would have encountered opposition in those states if it had sought to do so.

Too many people spout off a definition of secularism as "the principle of the separation of church and state." Typically, those same people – like the godless "Freedom from Religion" fascists in Madison, Wisconsin – twist those words around to make it something it is not. They embody the words of John Lennon's song, "Imagine." A doctoral dissertation could not cover all the many problems with that pagan paean, but let it suffice to say that when Lennon wrote "Imagine no possessions," he was living in a multi-million-dollar mansion, and the music video finds him playing his ridiculously expensive white Steinway piano that George Michael bought at auction for over two million dollars. Lennon wrote that it's easy if we try to imagine no religion, even as he lived in a time when godless communists slaughtered a hundred million of their own citizens.

As President Reagan put it so perfectly: "The Constitution was never meant to prevent people from praying; it's declared purpose was to protect their freedom to pray." Yet the "Freedom from Religion" crowd throw a tantrum over such things as taxpayers' children praying in taxpayer funded schools. Leftists get away with throwing their tantrums because too many people do not know the Constitution nor its historical precedents. Dear family, just wrap your minds around the fact that taxpayers' children praying in taxpayer funded schools was, in fact, Constitutional for roughly the first 175 years of our Country. Then realize that the ramifications of the rapid shift from this truth to the big lie of "Freedom from Religion" has resulted in the downfall of our culture and society. As a brilliant meme put it so well, "Bibles aren't allowed in schools anymore but are encouraged in prisons. If kids were allowed to read it at school, they might not end up in prison."

How do we sin regarding secularism? Simple. We sin every time we support, in word or deed, the big lie of "separation of church and state" according to the secularist model. We sin through any kind of voting for godless agendas. We also commit sins of omission when we fail to make a reasonable effort to be aware of, and fight against, these dark forces which are prevailing in our times. The many, versus the few, sin constantly in their ignorant and uninformed support – even cowardly support - for the godless left-wing agenda. This would include disregarding the unchanged and unchangeable truth regarding the five non-negotiables of Catholic morality, including abortion and same-sex unions.

WE ALSO COMMIT SINS OF OMISSION WHEN WE FAIL TO MAKE A REASONABLE EFFORT TO BE AWARE OF, AND FIGHT AGAINST, THESE DARK FORCES..."

What are we to do in a culture that literally assaults us (in words and in deeds) just for being Catholic and standing up for the unchanged and unchangeable truth? Firstly, recognize that we cannot be surprised by the hatred of the godless world. Jesus warned us: "If the world hates you, realize that it hated me first ... If they persecuted me, they will also persecute you ... And they will do all these things to you on account of my name, because they do not know the one who sent me" (John 15:18-21). No matter what hatred comes our way, we must stay attached to Jesus, who is the True Vine, lest we wither away. And we know what happens to those who choose to not stay attached to the vine: "Anyone who does not remain in me will be thrown out like a branch and wither; people will gather them and throw them into a fire and they will be burned" (John 15:6).

Dear family, buying into the big lie of secularism, and failure to intentionally let God's grace and wisdom openly direct and guide our public life, is a grave sin. You don't have to take my word for it. Jesus said, "Everyone who acknowledges me before others I will acknowledge before my heavenly Father. But whoever denies me before others, I will deny before my heavenly Father" (Matthew 10:32-33). We also know that standing up for our faith will alienate us from the godless because Jesus said that too: "Do you think that I have come to establish peace on the earth? No, I tell you, but rather division. From now on a household of five will be divided, three against two and two against three ...." (Luke 12:51-52).

Dear family, the left bludgeons anyone who brings faith into the public square, even priests, with the big lie of "separation of church and state." But prior to Lyndon Johnson's amendment and threat of taxation, faithful shepherds spoke up and spoke out against secular sin. Now, most everyone is a big coward, trembling in fear about being taxed. Please, dear family, honestly ask and answer two simple questions: Do we think the Father of Jesus Christ thinks it's a good idea that we cower in a corner because of oppressive secularism? Do we think Our Father thinks we should not openly bring Him into the public square? The answers are obvious. So are the consequences for how we answer those questions.

When Jesus said, "give to Caesar what is Caesar's, and give to God what is God's," the corollary is "don't give to Caesar what belongs to God." As it was, as it is, as it always will be: God first, last and always. So, let us always acknowledge God before men, and let us always openly apply our lives of faith in the public square.

Prayer of Reparation

My Lord and my God, we have allowed the temptation of the devil to move our hearts toward secularism. Countless times we have cowered to the prevailing leftist sentiment to imagine no religion, not just in public life, but even in private life. We are so immersed in temporal pleasures that we are blinded to our purpose in life, which is to know, love and serve God in this world so we can be with Him in the next. We intentionally justify leaving God out of our public lives because, after all, "freedom from religion" and their ilk have successfully inculcated us with the big lie of their false interpretation of the Constitution's Establishment Clause and insistence upon "separation of church and state." We fail to attribute the current chaos and anarchy of our times to the seeds of godlessness sown way back in the sixties when prayer was taken out of our taxpayer-funded schools. Ever since we have wittingly or unwittingly joined the side of the godless through our open or tacit acceptance of the big lie of secularism. We turn to You Lord, in our weakness, and beg Your forgiveness for our own secular attitudes – especially for our cowardice about speaking up and speaking out in the public square. We love You Lord, and we beg for the wisdom and strength to love You more. We know Lord, if You will it, it will be done. Trusting in You, we offer our prayer to You who live and reign forever and ever. Amen.

Prayer of Exorcism

Lord God of heaven and earth, in Your power and goodness, You created all things. You set a path for us to walk on and a way to an eternal relationship. By the strength of Your arm and Word of Your mouth, cast from Your Holy Church every fearful deceit of the devil. Drive from us manifestations of the demonic that oppress us and beckon us to secularism. Still the lying tongue of the devil and his forces so that we may act freely and faithfully to Your will. Send Your holy angels to cast out all influence that the demonic entities in charge of secularism have planted in Your Church. Free us, our families, our parish, our diocese, and our country from all trickery and deceit perpetrated by the devil and his hellish legions. Trusting in Your goodness Lord, we know if You will it, it will be done, in unity with Your Son and the Holy Spirit, One God forever and ever. Amen.

☖ DAY 30 CHECKLIST ☖

__ Prayer for Freedom from the Devil - pg. 255

__ Daily reflection and prayers

__ Litany of the day – pg. 256

__ Pray a Rosary (intention: exorcism of secularism) – pg.275

__ Divine Mercy Chaplet (in reparation for: sin due to secularism) – pg. 279

__ Spiritual or corporal work of mercy (see pg. 254)

__ Fast/abstain (according to level)

__ Exercise (according to level/ability)

__ Refrain from conventional media (only 1 hr. of social)

__ Examination of conscience (confession 1x this week)

Day 31
Freedom from MATERIALISM
By FR. WILLIAM PECKMAN

Back in 1985, Madonna nearly topped the Billboard 100 singing how she was "a material girl living in a material world." It seemed apropos for the eighties where herds of free-range yuppies thundered across the fruited plains alerting anyone who could hear them that too much stuff was never enough. Certainly, the USA is one of the wealthiest countries the world has ever seen. Even the bottom 20% of the economic strata in our country consumes more than the bottom 60% of the rest of the developed world. Our suburbs are full of McMansions stuffed with goods. At my worst, I had clothes in my closet that I owned for a couple years and never removed the price tags from. It used to be that the American Dream was about the ability to make something of yourself despite your economic class. Now, the American Dream is the house, the car, the possessions and so on. It can become a garish display.

Materialism comes from a very dark place. It is a godless place. Philosophically, materialism holds that all that is true is made up of material or comes from material interactions. Even the mind is subservient to the material world. In essence, all we have is what is measurable. No god. No heaven. No hell. No devil. Our life ends when we die. There is nothing beyond the grave. Hence, our only true happiness can be found in the accumulation of wealth, power, pleasure, and honor. Life becomes a mad dash of consumption and manipulation. Materialism is like a creeping vine; if not pulled up right away, it will insinuate itself into your life and choke off any fruit a relationship with God might have born.

Many people who consider themselves good Catholics can be functional materialists. A canary in the mineshaft is our attitude to the Day of the Lord, our attitude towards Sundays. If there is anywhere where the effects of materialism (and its twin serpent, secularism) are more greatly felt, it is in how we treat Sunday. In the last forty years Sunday has gone from the Day of the Lord to the hour of the Lord, that is, unless there is something more fun or important to do. Even for one day we cannot put down our material interests to address our spiritual need for prayer, communion, and rest. Apart from school, every other secular enterprise has gobbled up Sunday like a quickly eaten trifle. *ALERT* You are entering the slaughtering of sacred cows' zone!

Let's use the following conversation that I have had multiple times with parishioners: "My kid can't serve because he has a ball tournament this weekend." "And this tournament is both on Saturday night and SUNDAY MORNING?" "I know, Father, but he did make a

> MATERIALISM IS LIKE A CREEPING VINE; IF NOT PULLED UP RIGHT AWAY, IT WILL INSINUATE ITSELF INTO YOUR LIFE AND CHOKE OFF ANY FRUIT A RELATIONSHIP WITH GOD MIGHT HAVE BORN
>
> ""

commitment to the team. We will try to get to Mass at some time." Thinking to myself: *Hmm. I am sure what God meant by first fruits was really leftovers, but that's another discussion. Maybe we should talk about their commitment to God being of greater value.* "So why is going to this game so important?" "Because he needs extracurriculars to get into a good college?" "Why is that important?" "So he can get a good job." "Why is that important?" "So he can be successful and make a good salary." "Why is that important?" "So he can raise a family and live without financial worry." Me thinking to myself: *Hmm, no wonder my homilies on priestly vocations fall on deaf ears; but again, another time.* "May I quote Mark 8:6? 'What does it profit for man to gain the whole world yet forfeit their soul?' The third commandment is to keep holy the Sabbath, no? Is teaching your son that a ball game holds greater importance than the Day of the Lord a lesson you wish to teach to him?"

Teaching others, especially those placed in our care, that the material world and its prizes are of greater value than one's relationship with God and His people is a dangerous lesson. It is a contributory factor to the ever-plummeting attendance at Mass. If we will abandon Mass for worldly gain, will we not abandon anything of God to get ahead? The devil will grab his pom-poms and cheer you on that drive!

What Jesus calls for, instead of such an attachment to the material world, is a detachment from the material world. In the Sermon on the Mount, in the Gospel of Matthew, Jesus says, "Therefore I tell you, do not be anxious about your life, what you will eat or what you will drink, nor about your body, what you will put on. Is not life more than food, and the body more than clothing? Look at the birds of the air: they neither sow nor reap nor gather into barns, and yet your heavenly Father feeds them. Are you not of more value than they? And which of you by being anxious can add a single hour to his span of life? And why are you anxious about clothing? Consider the lilies of the field, how they grow: they neither toil nor spin, yet I tell you, even Solomon in all his glory was not arrayed like one of these." If this is the attitude Jesus tells us to have about the necessities of life, how much more does this apply to things like ballgames and other non-essential activities? I am not against sports. I am for right priorities. Faith helps us discern right priorities, considering that which is material, and hence passing, to be of lesser importance to the spiritual.

It is telling that in such a culture abstinence and fasting are seen as little more than misery-making exercises consigned to Lent. Are you aware that we are still not supposed to eat meat on any Friday? Outside of Lent, we can substitute something else. But Friday...all Fridays are days of abstinence. Fasting and abstinence are incredibly good ways of breaking ourselves from materialism.

I challenge you, dear reader, to start breaking apart from materialism with one simple step: make the Day of the Lord a day of rest and worship again. Maybe pick up some fasting and abstinence. We need to find ways to shout boldly our faith, "We need God before anything this world has to offer."

Prayer of Reparation

My Lord and my God, we have allowed the temptation of the devil to move our hearts to not see fulfillment in Your goodness. We have chased after earthly goals and trinkets as if they were more important. We have allowed material goals to supplant our relationship with You. We have expected You to be pleased with our neglect and half-heartedness. We have, at times, been a source of scandal for those searching through our sinfulness and rebellion to You. In our fear, we have allowed the ancient foe to advance. We turn to You Lord, in our sorrow and guilt, and beg Your forgiveness for our materialism. We beg for the grace of Your goodness to build up within us what You sought to build up in Your apostles in that tempest-tossed boat. We know, Lord, if You will it, it will be done. Trusting in You, we offer our prayer to You who live and reign forever and ever. Amen.

Prayer of Exorcism

Lord God of heaven and earth, in Your power and goodness, You created all things. You set a path for us to walk on and a way to an eternal relationship. By the strength of Your arm and Word of Your mouth, cast from Your Holy Church every fearful deceit of the devil. Drive from us manifestations of the demonic that oppress us and beckon us to materialism. Still the lying tongue of the devil and his forces so that we may act freely and faithfully to Your will. Send Your holy angels to cast out all influence that the demonic entities in charge of materialism have planted in Your Church. Free us, our families, our parish, our diocese, and our country from all trickery and deceit perpetrated by the devil and his hellish legions. Trusting in Your goodness Lord, we know if You will it, it will be done, in unity with Your Son and the Holy Spirit, one God, forever and ever. Amen.

☖DAY 31 CHECKLIST☖

__ Prayer for Freedom from the Devil - pg. 255

__ Daily reflection and prayers

__ Litany of the day – pg. 256

__ Pray a Rosary (intention: exorcism of materialism) – pg.275

__ Divine Mercy Chaplet (in reparation for: sin due to materialism) – pg. 279

__ Spiritual or corporal work of mercy (see pg. 254)

__ Fast/abstain (according to level)

__ Exercise (according to level/ability)

__ Refrain from conventional media (only 1 hr. of social)

__ Examination of conscience (confession 1x this week)

Day 32

Freedom from IRREVERENCE

By FR. RICHARD HEILMAN

It was on February 2, 1998, that I had the experience of a lifetime. It was my first ever Papal Mass, and this was with Pope John Paul II on the Feast of the Presentation. I went on sabbatical for two months with some priest friends to study in Rome. The priests studying received a beautiful, engraved invitation to the Papal Mass, and we were thrilled to be going.

There we were in St. Peter's Basilica in Rome, about to pray with the Vicar of Christ. As Mass began, glorious sacred music filled the Basilica...and my soul. Since it was a Papal Mass there was great attention given to precision, which struck me as "beautiful order," much like is seen with a military honor guard granting the highest respect to a fallen soldier. But it was more than that. While I had always loved the Mass, I felt, maybe for the first time, that we were truly "glorifying" God. On that day, February 2, 1998, I was profoundly changed.

That amazing experience simultaneously left me filled with regret. I began to ask myself, "What have I been doing?" I had spent the first ten years of my priesthood buying into the common (at the time) notion that if we created all kinds of trendy nuances to the Mass, while keeping it as whimsical and entertaining as possible, people would hear about how "cool" and "fun" and "with the times" we were and come running. We were treating the

Mass as a commodity that we needed to somehow market to the world. Worse than anything, I realized we were all but throwing out any sense of divinity, any sense of the supernatural. Where in all of this was any sense of awe and wonder in God's presence? Where was the sense of God's majesty? I realized, for the first time, we were gravely sinning in our irreverence before God.

Saint Francis of Assisi said, "Man should tremble, the world should quake, all Heaven should be deeply moved when the Son of God appears on the altar in the hands of the priest." Where was that in my "night club act" or "Broadway musical" entertainment-focused Masses? Irreverence!

I've come to understand that we have, throughout most of the Church, removed the very gateway into the Divine Life. I happen to agree with Pope St. Gregory the Great who, wanting to capture the spiritual dynamism of the gifts of the Holy Spirit, posited the following order: "Through the fear of the Lord, we rise to piety, from piety then to knowledge, from knowledge we derive strength, from strength counsel, with counsel we move toward understanding, and with intelligence toward wisdom and thus, by the sevenfold grace of the Spirit, there opens to us at the end of the ascent the entrance to the life of Heaven" ("Homiliae in Hiezechihelem Prophetam," II 7,7).

As you can see, the entry point to all the Gifts of the Holy Spirit is "Fear of the Lord." What is Fear of the Lord, also known as the Gift of Awe and Wonder? According to

Fr. John Hardon, Fear of the Lord "... inspires a person with profound respect for the majesty of God. Its corresponding effects are protection from sin through dread of offending the Lord, and a strong confidence in the power of His help. The fear of the Lord is not servile but filial. It is based on the selfless love of God, whom it shrinks from offending. Whereas in servile fear the evil dreaded is punishment; in filial fear it is the fear of doing anything contrary to the will of God. The gift of fear comprises three principal elements: a vivid sense of God's greatness, a lively sorrow for the least faults committed, and a vigilant care in avoiding occasions of sin. It is expressed in prayer of the Psalmist, 'My whole being trembles before you, Your ruling fills me with fear'" (Psalm 119:120).

Fear of the Lord is the entry point; this is the "trigger" that ignites all the other gifts of the Holy Spirit. Without this trigger, we are prone to reduce our faith/religion to merely another organization that has a sense of social

FEAR OF THE LORD IS THE ENTRY POINT; THIS IS THE "TRIGGER" THAT IGNITES ALL THE OTHER GIFTS OF THE HOLY SPIRIT

responsibility. Jesus is then reduced to a historic figure to emulate. Mass is just a social gathering that many may say (without saying), "it had better have good entertainment if You are going to make me endure this for an hour." So then, why not just throw on our worst recreational attire for Mass, and get in line to grab Jesus like we're reaching for a potato chip? Where is the desire to be filled with the supernatural power of grace?

St. Bernard said, "For I have learnt for a fact that nothing so effectively obtains, retains and regains grace, as that we should always be found not high-minded before God, but filled with holy fear."

Fr. John Hardon wrote: "St. Thomas Aquinas believed that man is more than a composite of body and soul, that his is nothing less than elevated to a supernatural order which participates, as far as a creature can, in the very nature of God. Accordingly, a person in the state of grace, or divine friendship, possesses certain enduring powers, the infused virtues and gifts, that raise him to an orbit of existence as far above nature as heaven is above earth, and that give him abilities of thought and operation that are literally born, not of the will of flesh nor of the will of man, but of God."

Do you see why Satan is winning?! He is in the supernatural realm using supernatural weapons, while we have surrendered ours. We seem to be choosing, instead, an irreverent, secular (anti-supernatural) version of religion. I honestly believe this goes to the very root of our problems. Unless, and until, we see a worldwide movement within our Church to restore reverence in the Holy Sacrifice of the Mass, that assists us in becoming predisposed to receive the gateway Holy Spirit Gift of Awe and Wonder, Satan will continue to have an easy-time with us. Until then, Satan is eating our lunch!

Prayer of Reparation

My Lord and my God, we have allowed the temptation of the devil to move our hearts toward fearfully allowing the spread of irreverence throughout our Catholic Church. We have fallen into this widespread irreverence when we have not lived up to the call of our baptism to, day-by-day, deepen our love and faith in You. We have been too easily swayed by the poor example of irreverence, in churches everywhere, and have not encouraged a deeper sense of supernatural faith. In our weakness, we have allowed the ancient foe to advance. We turn to You Lord, in our sorrow and guilt, and beg Your forgiveness for any of our own irreverence or our lack of resolve to lift souls out of this spiritual malaise. We beg for the grace of Your goodness to build up within us the strength and endurance to be this visible light of fervent faith in You. We know, Lord, if You will it, it will be done. Trusting in You, we offer our prayer to You who live and reign forever and ever. Amen.

Prayer of Exorcism

Lord God of heaven and earth, in Your power and goodness, You created all things. You set a path for us to walk on and a way to an eternal relationship. By the strength of Your arm and Word of Your mouth, cast from Your Holy Church every fearful deceit of the devil. Drive from us manifestations of the demonic that oppress us and beckon us to irreverence. Still the lying tongue of the devil and his forces so that we may act freely and faithfully to do Your will. Send Your holy angels to cast out all influence that the demonic entities in charge of irreverence have planted in Your Church. Free us, our families, our parish, our diocese, and our country from all trickery and deceit perpetrated by the devil and his hellish legions. Trusting in Your goodness Lord, we know if You will it, it will be done, in unity with Your Son and the Holy Spirit, One God forever and ever. Amen.

⌂ DAY 32 CHECKLIST ⌂

__ Prayer for Freedom from the Devil - pg. 255

__ Daily reflection and prayers

__ Litany of the day – pg. 256

__ Pray a Rosary (intention: exorcism of irreverence) – pg.275

__ Divine Mercy Chaplet (in reparation for: sin due to irreverence) – pg. 279

__ Spiritual or corporal work of mercy (see pg. 254)

__ Fast/abstain (according to level)

__ Exercise (according to level/ability)

__ Refrain from conventional media (only 1 hr. of social)

__ Examination of conscience (confession 1x this week)

Day 33
Freedom from THEFT
By FR. JAMES ALTMAN

Dear family, Our Father gave us the Ten Commandments for a reason, a good reason. Few people will do it, but we all should look in the mirror and say, "MY Father gave me Ten Commandments because He knew very well I, myself, needed such COMMANDS – not suggestions – because otherwise I would tend to misbehave." After all, if we all were greatly inclined to holiness, we would not have needed those ten in the first place. In fact – and again, few like to admit it – Our Father pretty much had us pegged as to the main areas we would sin.

So, He gave us these commands, like stripes along the highway, to keep us within the boundaries of the narrow road to Heaven. To stray outside those boundaries – to disobey those Commandments – to SIN – well, welcome to the broad road to destruction. Sometimes there are immediate consequences, like running into the ditch of sin, hitting a tree, and dying. Other times there are less immediate consequences. We might "get away" with doing something – or so we erroneously think. Like that secular hymn to Santa, Our Father does know

> SO, HE GAVE US THESE COMMANDS, LIKE STRIPES ALONG THE HIGHWAY, TO KEEP US WITHIN THE BOUNDARIES OF THE NARROW ROAD TO HEAVEN
>
> 99

when we've been bad or good, so be good for goodness' sake.

Life itself tends to have consequences when we violate those Ten Commandments, when we sin. If we sin in smaller matters, maybe those consequences will be like straying over the "chatter-bumps" intended to alert us when we stray onto or over the highway stripes. Maybe we will get away with texting while driving most of the time. That's what makes it so dangerous. Without immediate consequences we are lulled into a false sense of security, we are emboldened, until that day when our distracted driving does result in a real accident and we and others are maimed or killed. So it is with venial sins. The consequences are not immediate or are minor, so we are emboldened to continue and push the envelope further. That is such dangerous ground. Sin causes darkness in our souls, and the more we sin, the more it gets dark, dark, dark in there. It gets darker and darker until the time when we cross the line into grave sin and do not even recognize it for what it is. Then, dear family, we have most certainly chosen to drive down the broad road to destruction.

Dear family, I say all this because too many people do not appreciate Commandment #7, thou shalt not steal. Other words for stealing include "theft" and "larceny." In the secular world, theft is often defined as the unauthorized taking of property from another with the intent to permanently deprive them of it. Within this definition lie two key elements: a) a taking of someone else's property, and b) the requisite intent to deprive the victim of the property permanently.

As an aside, it permanently leaves out "unauthorized borrowing" – but just try and tell the store that you only were borrowing something you shoplifted! Similarly, if we put on our thinking caps, it just "doesn't fly" when a criminal alien suggests his "unauthorized entry" simply was a moment of "undocumented immigration." Our Federal Government – and every government on the face of this planet – has immigration commandments for a purpose. Get it straight, dear family: illegal aliens, who enter unauthorized, are thieves who have just stolen from every other citizen of this country, and no amount of left-wing-lib-editing of the terminology to "undocumented" can change that.

Understand this, dear family, Our Father had to COMMAND us not to steal precisely because we were inclined to steal. We were inclined to take that which was not ours. And the more we take, the more darkened our souls are to the reality and the gravity of the theft. Eventually, we get to the point of not even realizing we are taking. That is when we are blithely driving down the very center of the road to destruction.

Dear family, most of us know what does or does not belong to us. You don't need me to tell you that taking what is not yours is a sin, and that there will be consequences now or in eternity. You know this. For today, please recognize that many do NOT know this, or do not care. I do not believe for a second that all those rioters, looters, burners, and shooters are unaware that what they are taking or destroying is not theirs. They just do not care. They are lawless, which means – get this straight – they are godless. When you disregard the law and disregard God, it really is just that simple. Let us recognize it for what it is. This godlessness can be less evident, like when all those people took over the Wisconsin State Capital in a "protest," ultimately causing about seven million dollars in costs and damages – all paid for by the Badger taxpayers. Dear family, apart from the fact that many of them were teachers taking unauthorized leave and stealing time from the parents and students, they literally stole from every taxpayer every penny of costs and damages. They. Are. Thieves.

While I do not need to define taking of anything tangible, like a candy bar from Kwik Trip or a Wrangler from the Jeep dealership, the above example of the teachers stealing intangible time is instructive for another type of theft of which so many are clueless. For today, let us relate theft of intangible time by relating Commandment #7, "Thou shalt not steal," to Commandment #3, "Keep Holy the Lord's Day." The commandment was a day. That means 24 hours. I sometimes say it this way, "God commanded us to keep holy the DAY. That means 24 hours. Commandment #3 does not say 'keep holy the Lord's 55 minutes and get mad if father's homily is a little long!" A day is a day, and a day has 24 hours. Remember that bit about how if we sin our soul gets darker until it gets really dark? All those people who cannot be bothered to show up for the Holy Sacrifice of the Mass on Sunday – they commit grave sin because they have stolen God's time. Usually, it does not happen all at once. Usually, they start by playing fast and loose with just some of the 24 hours – doing unnecessary work or making someone else do unnecessary work by shopping or eating out on Sunday. They start down that very slippery slope until one day – boom, they find any excuse good enough to blow off their Sunday OBLIGATION. That will not end well for them. If they do not want to be with God on Sunday, they will not be with Him in eternity. Period.

> ALL OF THOSE PEOPLE WHO CANNOT BE BOTHERED TO SHOW UP FOR THE HOLY SACRIFICE OF THE MASS ON SUNDAY – THEY COMMIT GRAVE SIN BECAUSE THEY HAVE STOLEN GOD'S TIME
>
> 99

Dear family, most of us – excluding the rioters, looters, burners, and shooters - know that we should not steal tangible things. How about for today let us ponder how so many of us steal intangible things – like time – like God's time? As part of our next confession, let us examine our consciences and ask ourselves how much time we have stolen. That is an important examination, dear family, because stealing time makes us thieves. To help with that examination, let us ask ourselves if we have made it a point to do what Jesus told us to do: spend an hour a day with our Lord in this life, so we really can spend an eternity with

Him in the next. Then let us in these troubled, troubled times resolve to be free from our attachment to time, and to start giving back to the Lord one hour for every 23 other hours of the day He gives us.

Prayer of Reparation

My Lord and my God, we have allowed the temptation of the devil to move our hearts toward theft. Maybe our greatest theft is the theft of time, our stealing from the Lord what really is His time. We are so immersed in temporal pleasures that we are blinded to our purpose in life, which is to know, love and serve God in this world so we can be with Him in the next. Serving takes time, and so many are so stingy with their time. We intentionally justify leaving God out of our daily lives because we have so many other priorities other than God. So often we drive so far outside the God-defined narrow lines of life that we do not even recognize we are on the broad road to destruction. We turn to You Lord, in our weakness, and beg Your forgiveness for our own theft of time – especially for the times we have not even kept Your day holy, all 24 hours of Your day. We love You Lord, and we beg for the wisdom and strength to love You more. We know, Lord, if You will it, it will be done. Trusting in You, we offer our prayer to You who live and reign forever and ever. Amen.

Prayer of Exorcism

Lord God of heaven and earth, in Your power and goodness, You created all things. You set a path for us to walk on and a way to an eternal relationship. By the strength of Your arm and Word of Your mouth, cast from Your Holy Church every fearful deceit of the devil. Drive from us manifestations of the demonic that oppress us and beckon us to theft. Still the lying tongue of the devil and his forces so that we may act freely and faithfully to Your will. Send Your holy angels to cast out all influence that the demonic entities in charge of theft have planted in Your Church. Free us, our families, our parish, our diocese, and our country from all trickery and deceit perpetrated by the devil and his hellish legions. Trusting in Your goodness Lord, we know if You will it, it will be done, in unity with Your Son and the Holy Spirit, One God forever and ever. Amen.

🔔 DAY 33 CHECKLIST 🔔

__ Prayer for Freedom from the Devil - pg. 255

__ Daily reflection and prayers

__ Litany of the day – pg. 256

__ Pray a Rosary (intention: exorcism of theft) – pg.275

__ Divine Mercy Chaplet (in reparation for: sin due to theft) – pg. 279

__ Spiritual or corporal work of mercy (see pg. 254)

__ Fast/abstain (according to level)

__ Exercise (according to level/ability)

__ Refrain from conventional media (only 1 hr. of social)

__ Examination of conscience (confession 1x this week)

Day 34
Freedom from RELATIVISM

By FR. WILLIAM PECKMAN

For years, I have tried to do a class with my seventh and eighth grade religion classes on some form of critical and analytical thinking. One of the first things I teach them is the difference between subjective and objective truth. I do this because they are entering a society that is more and more hostile to the concept of objective truth.

The easiest way to tell the two apart is that objective truth is something that is true on its own merit (it does not need my opinion to prove its veracity), whereas subjective truth is something that is true by my criteria (opinion). Our society has embraced relativism as a natural outgrowth of its hostility to true faith. In fact (and I say this as a former agnostic), relativism is the grand prize of godlessness: I get to decide for myself what is good and evil, moral and immoral, and right or wrong. Relativism gives me the false pretense of being my own God. It is biting into the apple at Eden.

Relativism bases itself in our emotions being more important than our rational thinking when it comes to decision making and the pursuit of truth. Since everything is subjective, truth is what I feel it is based on my own perceived emotional needs and passions. My passions and emotions are the filters through which I define my reality. So, what happens when my reality does not line up with your reality? You must be wrong and you should align yourself with my reality. If you don't, then I will call you intolerant, and if you try to express an opinion contrary to mine, then I will shout you down. Does this sound familiar?

Our society is rife with relativism. It has long trumped faith; now it trumps science and empirical evidence. If I am a male and feel that I am not, you must accept it. If I am sexually attracted to…well…anything, you must accept it. If I believe that I should get everything for free, you must give it. Progressivism is relativistic. It is why everything: every belief, every thought, and every word, must be a reflection of itself. It is the powertrain of narcissism.

Our Church has been rocked with relativism. It shows up in the cleric who has come to his own conclusion that a teaching is antiquated (say artificial birth control), and therefore ceases to discuss it or teaches contrary to it (and also in the one who believes it but lacks the intestinal fortitude to instruct his flock). It shows up in the "I am Catholic but…" attitude that CINO (Catholic In Name Only) politicians and academics like to hide behind. They pretend they are Catholics in good standing to get your vote or your ear. I have seen it in so called "celebrity priests" who talk a good game but allow the press to go to their heads. They start thinking they are above the teachings us ordinary folk must follow, and scandal soon ensues. I still maintain that a cleric must have a high degree of relativism to prey on their flock (or allow the predation to happen), AND still even so much as touch the Blessed

Sacrament, let alone say Mass. It is the food that feeds the attitude that the purpose of the Mass is "getting something out of it."

In John 14, from the Farewell Discourse, Jesus says "I am the way, the truth, and the life" (John 14:6). When preaching on this passage, I always remind people that articles matter. Jesus doesn't use the indefinite article as in "I am a way, a truth, and a life." He uses the definite article. Jesus, His teachings, and the Gospel are not just one man's opinion or an option among other possible options. His words are not co-equal with worldly or secular wisdom. Since He alone is the Second Person of the Trinity made flesh who dwelt amongst us, His words and teachings carry a unique and singular authority. By the same notion, the Church He set up is the caretaker and keeper of the keys to that same singular truth. Because someone else (or even our own self) has come up with an alternative, does NOT make that alternative true or co-equal with the truth that is Jesus Christ.

So, what is the antidote to such a potent poison? Humility, humility, humility! In humility we see the truth. In humility we see our own paltry attempts at truth as nothing before God. In humility we bow our heads to God's wisdom and power. In humility  we see truth clearly and can act rightly and justly. Since humility doesn't consider "What's in it for me?" it gives us clarity of vision and a hunger to act in truth. It helps us see relativism for the self-serving and ultimately (and eternally) self-destructive drug it is. Humility gives us the ability to move beyond ourselves and become genuinely loving.

My brothers and sisters, we do well to cultivate humility even when such cultivation upends our lives and forces conversion. This is a good thing. We would do well to do this now before it is too late. We might be able to fool ourselves and even those around us. We might be able to bully our neighbor and shout down those who disagree with us. Be that as it may, we will not be able to defend, shout down, nor bully God into seeing our way and giving us the reward set aside for those who allowed themselves to be conformed to His image and likeness. For after saying He is the way, the truth, and the life, Jesus tells us that no one comes to the Father except through Him. We do well to listen.

Prayer of Reparation

My Lord and my God, we have allowed the temptation of the devil to move our hearts to not see fulfillment in Your truth. We have chased after earthly goals and trinkets as if they were more important. We have allowed self-serving and self-destructive passions to supplant obedience to You. We have expected You to be pleased with our neglect and half-heartedness. We have, at times, been a source of scandal for those searching through our sinfulness and rebellion to You. In our fear, we have allowed the ancient foe to advance. We turn to You Lord, in our sorrow and guilt, and beg Your forgiveness for our relativism. We beg for the grace of Your goodness to build up within us what You sought to build up in Your apostles in that tempest-tossed boat. We know, Lord, if You will it, it will be done. Trusting in You, we offer our prayer to You who live and reign forever and ever. Amen

Prayer of Exorcism

Lord God of heaven and earth, in Your power and goodness, You created all things. You set a path for us to walk on and a way to an eternal relationship. By the strength of Your arm and Word of Your mouth, cast from Your Holy Church every fearful deceit of the devil. Drive from us manifestations of the demonic that oppress us and beckon us to relativism. Still the lying tongue of the devil and his forces so that we may act freely and faithfully to Your will. Send Your holy angels to cast out all influence that the demonic entities in charge of relativism have planted in Your Church. Free us, our families, our parish, our diocese, and our country from all trickery and deceit perpetrated by the devil and his hellish legions. Trusting in Your goodness Lord, we know if You will it, it will be done, in unity with Your Son and the Holy Spirit, One God forever and ever. Amen.

♤ DAY 34 CHECKLIST ♤

___ Prayer for Freedom from the Devil - pg. 255

___ Daily reflection and prayers

___ Litany of the day – pg. 256

___ Pray a Rosary (intention: exorcism of relativism) – pg.275

___ Divine Mercy Chaplet (in reparation for: sin due to relativism) – pg. 279

___ Spiritual or corporal work of mercy (see pg. 254)

___ Fast/abstain (according to level)

___ Exercise (according to level/ability)

___ Refrain from conventional media (only 1 hr. of social)

___ Examination of conscience (confession 1x this week)

Day 35
Freedom from CHILDISHNESS
By FR. RICHARD HEILMAN

Psychology has always been an area of interest for me. In fact, I graduated from college with a degree in psychology. Since then, I have become very suspicious of the APA (American Psychological Association) as they have been, quite obviously, infiltrated by so-called "progressives" (See my reflection above on "Freedom from Pride" to discover the problem with progressives). These people, among other things, crave notoriety for so-called "new knowledge" that, up to now, has not been commonly held.

Consequently, the behavioral "science" coming from the APA has become muddled. Behaviors formerly seen as disorders, are now considered normal behavior by the progressive APA. So, for example, grown men must now be allowed to share bathrooms with little girls. And watch out for the new movement looking to normalize pedophilia…it's coming fast! I will get back to the APA shortly.

In the context of *Let Freedom Ring*, we talk about the spiritual deficiencies of values, virtues, and morals in our culture. In many ways, these spiritual deficiencies intersect with psychological deficiencies.

When observing the condition of our culture, it is clear it shows signs of an alarming growth of emotional childishness, which is not unlike a lack of spiritual maturity.

More and more people have, as renowned psychologist, Dr. Susan Heitler states, "reached chronological adulthood without having mastered the core elements of adult emotional functioning."

Dr. Heitler points to 10 signs of a childish adult - See how many of these you recognize in the mob's temper tantrums:

1. Emotional escalations
2. Blaming
3. Lies
4. Name-calling
5. Impulsivity
6. Need to be the center of attention
7. Bullying
8. Budding narcissism ("It's all about me." In the eyes of a narcissist, no one else counts. If they don't get their way, they may result to pouting or bullying in order to do so.)
9. Immature defenses (the tendency to attack anyone who expresses a differing viewpoint- ex. cancel culture).
10. No observing ego (the inability to see, acknowledge, and learn from their mistakes).

These behaviors are not unique to the mob in the streets, as it is replete in the mainstream media; look at Hollywood and the far too many emotionally childish politicians. In today's culture, we are treading in completely new territory. While some may say we have always seen immature adults, the degree to which we are witnessing this today is massive and unprecedented. It is no longer about right vs. left; it is about mature adults vs. childish adults.

It used to be that grownups could disagree with each other and calmly work out their differences, while listening, considering each other's viewpoints, and maintaining a level of respect for each other. Now, in this new milieu of widespread emotional immaturity, those of us playing like adults are living in fear of being assaulted by the temper tantrums of those who act like misbehaving children (blaming, lies, name-calling, bullying, attacking, etc.).

Consider what has happened, just recently, in my neck of the woods, but it is emblematic of what is going on everywhere in America. A friend recently had his car keyed because he had a pro-life bumper sticker. Another friend had his house damaged for flying the Thin Blue Line flag that honors police. Our downtown is boarded up and painted with graffiti because the mob's temper tantrums include violence, looting, tearing down statues, and burning down businesses. In the 2020 election year, few dared to display yard signs or bumper stickers for the candidate the childish didn't like, for fear of being attacked. Many were scared to associate themselves in any way with the "wrong" candidate (in the eyes of the childish), for fear of being assaulted, calumniated, or even fired from their jobs. A friend of mine chose not to run for public office over worries that he and his family would be targeted by the childish mob. And the examples go on and on and on.

How did we get here? The simple answer is poor parenting, or even absent parenting. I recall when the

Nouveau Parenting movement began - mostly spurred on by the new "woke" and "progressive" APA. Parents were told to cease disciplining their children, for fear of traumatizing them. Meanwhile, organizations started handing out participation trophies just for showing up, because disappointment over not earning a prize could be damaging to a kid's self-esteem. What. A. Colossal. Disaster!

Parents who coddle their children are, quite frankly, stunting their emotional maturation. This is certainly not how our perfect parent, God, parents us. Salvation history is replete with examples where God, having first tried to inspire us, resorts to allowing us to go through challenges. The opposition we face in those challenges, impels us to "raise our game" - to mature. Left to

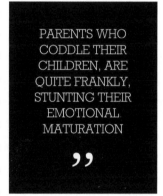

PARENTS WHO CODDLE THEIR CHILDREN, ARE QUITE FRANKLY, STUNTING THEIR EMOTIONAL MATURATION

our spiritual immaturity, we are prone to behave as spoiled children do. We expect God to give us everything we want, including heaven, without ever needing to humbly obey, express our gratitude, or work hard for it; we feel we are just entitled to it. We'd rather not know of such adult concepts as, "Effort brings reward."

Jesus said to his disciples, "Whoever wishes to come after me must deny himself, take up his cross, and follow me" (Matt 16:24). These are not the words of someone who coddles with participation "trophies." This is the Son of God telling us to "GROW UP and BE A MAN! (or WOMAN!)"

In the military, they put it this way, "It never gets easier, you just get better."

Prayer of Reparation

My Lord and my God, we have allowed the temptation of the devil to move our hearts toward fearfully allowing the spread of childishness throughout our culture and our Catholic Church. We have fallen into this widespread childishness when we have not lived up to the call of our baptism to, day-by-day, deepen our love and faith in You. We have been too easily swayed by the poor example of childishness, in churches everywhere, and have not encouraged a deeper sense of supernatural faith. In our weakness, we have allowed the ancient foe to advance. We turn to You Lord, in our sorrow and guilt, and beg Your forgiveness for any of our own childishness or our lack of resolve to lift souls out of this lack of spiritual maturity. We beg for the grace of Your goodness to build up within us the strength and endurance to be this visible light of fervent faith in You. We know Lord, if You will it, it will be done. Trusting in You, we offer our prayer to You who live and reign forever and ever. Amen.

Prayer of Exorcism

Lord God of heaven and earth, in Your power and goodness, You created all things. You set a path for us to walk on and a way to an eternal relationship. By the strength of Your arm and Word of Your mouth, cast from Your Holy Church every fearful deceit of the devil. Drive from us manifestations of the demonic that oppress us and beckon us to childishness. Still the lying tongue of the devil and his forces so that we may act freely and faithfully to do Your will. Send Your holy angels to cast out all influence that the demonic entities in charge of childishness have planted in Your Church. Free us, our families, our parish, our diocese, and our country from all trickery and deceit perpetrated by the devil and his hellish legions. Trusting in Your goodness Lord, we know if You will it, it will be done, in unity with Your Son and the Holy Spirit, One God forever and ever. Amen.

🔔 DAY 35 CHECKLIST 🔔

__ Prayer for Freedom from the Devil - pg. 255

__ Daily reflection and prayers

__ Litany of the day – pg. 256

__ Pray a Rosary (intention: exorcism of childishness) – pg.275

__ Divine Mercy Chaplet (in reparation for: sin due to childishness) – pg. 279

__ Spiritual or corporal work of mercy (see pg. 254)

__ Fast/abstain (according to level)

__ Exercise (according to level/ability)

__ Refrain from conventional media (only 1 hr. of social)

__ Examination of conscience (confession 1x this week)

Day 36
Freedom from AVARICE
By FR. JAMES ALTMAN

Dear family, avarice is a synonym of greed. It is one of the Seven Deadly Sins. Some distinguish between avarice and greed, essentially implying that avarice is like greed-on-steroids. No matter which word we care to use, both regard an excessive or inordinate desire of gain or wealth; a selfish or excessive desire for more than is needed or deserved, especially of money, wealth, food, or other possessions.

Avarice has a long if uncomplicated history in English. Chaucer in his 14th-century *The Parson's Tale* compared avarice with covetise, a now obsolete word that means "covetousness" ("Covetise is to covet such things as thou hast not; and avarice is to withhold and keep such things as thou hast, without rightful need"—743), and Shakespeare uses it in Macbeth ("With this there grows / In my most ill-composed affection such / A stanchless avarice that, were I king, / I should cut off the nobles for their lands, / Desire his jewels and this other's house: / And my more-having would be as a sauce / To make me hunger more"—IV.iii.76-82).

As he always seemed to do, the brilliant Shakespeare got it spot-on. "My more-having would be as a sauce to make me hunger more." Remember the life lesson of Adam and Eve, summarized as "Nothing is ever enough." Remember how they had everything, but it wasn't enough?

That really is the problem with avarice – nothing ever is enough, but only makes one want more.

Apart from that issue, of course, are the Gospel teachings on what happens when avarice runs amok. Remember the rich man who had a bountiful harvest. "Oh!" says he, "I will tear down my smaller barns and build bigger barns!" Not a good idea. First, it sounds pretty wasteful to tear down perfectly good barns. When we hear about wealthy people buying homes and tearing them down to build bigger ones, don't we suppose those people have never read Jesus' parable? Second, Jesus makes it clear – crystal clear – what Almighty God thinks about that kind of stuff; "You fool, this night your life will be demanded of you; and the things you have prepared, to whom will they belong?" (Luke 12:20). And then Jesus delivers the coup de grace: "Thus will it be for the one who stores up treasure for himself but is not rich in what matters to God" (Luke 12:21). And as if that weren't bad enough, there is the little problem about that camel trying to get through the eye of the needle.

Ok, so we know all that; but, here is something few look in the mirror and contemplate. Yeah, we might not be longing for Aaron Spelling's Hollywood mansion, but we all have it rather good. In fact, many of us tend to live beyond "our means." Here's an example ...

When I was teaching in the high school, I would ask the juniors or seniors, "How much do you think you will make when you get out of college?" The answers ranged from a low of about 40k, to a high of around 80k. The thing is, it did not matter what number with which I started, when we subtracted a mere 1/3 for taxes, and then subtracted the things upon which they themselves said they would spend "their" money – housing (I mentioned to them the hidden extras like furniture, appliances, bedding, towels, laundry soap, homeowners' or renters' insurance), auto (I mentioned to them the hidden extras like auto insurance, gas, oil changes), student-loans, cell phones, cable/internet, pizza on Friday – when we got done, both high and low incomes were at least 10-20% "in the red!" The thing is, the more we make, the more we live in nicer housing, drive fancier newer cars, and get the newest latest iPhones. And then I would bring up "Christmas and birthday gifts" - where their money was spent on someone other than themselves! They thought about it and sure enough, deeper into the red they went. And then – here it comes, dear family – about this point I would say "Hey! What's missing here?! I don't see any almsgiving, no giving back to God for all He has given you. There is nothing here for Church and charity."

Dear family, I wasn't being mean. I only was pointing out the reality that pretty much all of us are infected with an avaricious "living large" mentality. We all live in the biggest barns that the banks will loan us the money to buy. We all tend to drive the best vehicles the lenders will loan us the money to buy. And we all tend to have decent cell phones, cable, and internet. And pretty much none of us are going hungry when the CDC tells us: "During 2011–

2014, the age-adjusted prevalence of obesity was 38.3% among women and 34.3% among men."

Dear family, we all suffer from avarice. Whatever level our income might be, we long for more. And what's even worse about all this, is that we even will blow off the 3rd Commandment so – really, how many times have we heard this? – "I'm working or putting in some overtime on Sunday."

As to that last thing, working on Sundays, I also used to ask the high schoolers if they would sell their soul to the devil for a million bucks. "Oh, NO, father," they would say. I would up the ante to ten million dollars. "Oh, NO, father," they would say. Finally, I went all out – "Would you sell your soul to the devil for a billion dollars?! You could have the house, the boat and the car, and still have 999 million to live off the interest!" "Oh, NO, father," they all would say. At that point, I would tell them they were dead wrong - they would sell their souls to work on Sunday for minimum wage at Shopko or the IGA, all because they "needed" money for clothes, cells, car insurance or gas.

This analysis does not apply just to high schoolers. It applies to all adults who – whether they realize it or not – suffer from a level of avarice that takes away not just from the amount of

WHATEVER LEVEL OUR INCOME MIGHT BE, WE LONG FOR MORE

"

money they should be tithing, but also takes away from the

most valuable time we are commanded to give back to God by keeping the Lord's Day holy.

Dear family, I'm not sure how to tell anyone to fix this problem. I cannot give specific advice for anyone because the circumstances differ for each one of us. What I can say is that each one of us, myself included, really needs to ask ourselves, are we giving back to God what is God's? Or are we, because of the deadly sin of avarice, keeping way too much for ourselves?

Prayer of Reparation

My Lord and my God, we have allowed the temptation of the devil to move our hearts toward avarice. We are greedy. We recognize our avarice in the many things we own – including all the stuff we bought with borrowed money. At times we justify our avarice so much that we do not see ourselves in the Gospel parables of the man who planned to tear down his barns. At times we do not recognize in ourselves that we are the rich man who will have a harder time making it through the Gates of Heaven than a camel through the eye of a needle. We immerse ourselves in so many temporal goods that we do not even recognize we are living large with what we want, which is way more than what we truly need. We even justify leaving God out of our very budgets because we just cannot afford it! So often we just do not recognize our avarice. We turn to You Lord, in our weakness, and beg Your forgiveness for our avarice, and especially for all the times we have forfeited time with You for time to labor so we may indeed "live large." We love You Lord, and we beg for the wisdom and strength to love You more. We know, Lord, if You will it, it will be done. Trusting in You, we offer our prayer to You who live and reign forever and ever. Amen.

Prayer of Exorcism

Lord God of heaven and earth, in Your power and goodness, You created all things. You set a path for us to walk on and a way to an eternal relationship. By the strength of Your arm and Word of Your mouth, cast from Your Holy Church every fearful deceit of the devil. Drive from us manifestations of the demonic that oppress us and beckon us to avarice. Still the lying tongue of the devil and his forces so that we may act freely and faithfully to Your will. Send Your holy angels to cast out all influence that the demonic entities in charge of avarice have planted in Your Church. Free us, our families, our parish, our diocese, and our country from all trickery and deceit perpetrated by the devil and his hellish legions. Trusting in Your goodness Lord, we know if You will it, it will be done, in unity with Your Son and the Holy Spirit, one God, forever and ever. Amen.

🔔 DAY 36 CHECKLIST 🔔

__ Prayer for Freedom from the Devil - pg. 255

__ Daily reflection and prayers

__ Litany of the day – pg. 256

__ Pray a Rosary (intention: exorcism of avarice) – pg.275

__ Divine Mercy Chaplet (in reparation for: sin due to avarice) – pg. 279

__ Spiritual or corporal work of mercy (see pg. 254)

__ Fast/abstain (according to level)

__ Exercise (according to level/ability)

__ Refrain from conventional media (only 1 hr. of social)

__ Examination of conscience (confession 1x this week)

Day 37
Freedom from GOSSIP
By FR. WILLIAM PECKMAN

On the old TV show *Bewitched,* there was a character named Mrs. Cravitz. Mrs. Cravitz sat by her blinds, watching outside for anything that didn't look normal. and would yell for her husband, Abner, every time she had something to report. If I were to pick a character that dominates the media now, it would be Mrs. Cravitz. We seemingly can't get enough gossip. The more famous the person, the more gossip. We have TV shows dedicated to celebrity gossip. We have websites dedicated to gossip. We have collectively taken the attitude that, "if you have nothing nice to say about anybody, come sit next to me."

The type of gossip I am talking about is what we call calumny and detraction. According to the *Catechism of the Catholic Church,* one who commits detraction is one who "without objectively valid reason, discloses another's faults and failings to persons who did not know them" and one who commits calumny is one who, "by remarks contrary to the truth, harms the reputation of others and gives occasion for false judgments concerning them" (CCC 2477).

Gossip is an act in which we seek to destroy the reputation of another person for whatever reason. Many times, gossip is a passive-aggressive form of vengeance. Sometimes gossip is done for pure blood-sport. This is especially true in politics. Gossip is done as a way of distracting people from the problems the gossiper has. Sometimes it is done to position oneself as better in the eyes of others, to get some worldly prize. Whatever reason it is done, it is a sin against charity.

Both calumny and detraction rely on a third leg for this dismal and demonic trifecta: rash judgement. The *Catechism* refers to one who commits rash judgment as one "who, even tacitly, assumes as true, without sufficient foundation, the moral fault of a neighbor" (CCC 2477). To engage in gossip is to act as if we expect

SOMETIMES IT IS DONE TO POSITION ONESELF AS BETTER IN THE EYES OF OTHERS, TO GET SOME WORLDLY PRIZE

"

the absolute worst, in motivations and actions, from the person being gossiped about. Furthermore, it is a sin against Jesus' teaching. In Matthew 18:15-20, gossiping about one who has sinned, or appears to have sinned, is NOT one of the steps of fraternal correction. As followers of Christ, we are to seek the conversion of those who have sinned, not their public ridicule. It is most difficult to inspire conversion through destroying another person's good name.

This becomes mortally sinful with lies, when either through unwarranted speculation or outright maleficence, the gossip is not true. One then sins against the 8th Commandment: "Thou shall not bear false witness".

We see this in the Church with great regularity. Many times, in Catholic social media and in the blogosphere, we see stories that are little more than exercises in rash judgment, detraction, and calumny. As a priest, I would say that gossip is all too often an occupational hazard among clerics. I know I can justify it from time to time. I can sound like a not-to-be-named nineties TV character who said, "I don't gossip. Maybe sometimes I find out things or hear something and I pass that information on... You know...kind of like a public service." We can make all kinds of excuses for our gossip. It is sinful.

People come to me and ask, "When is it considered gossip?" My first question is, "Have you talked to that person about this?" That would be the first step in the scriptural method for fraternal correction. Second, I ask if you are seeking that person's conversion or humiliation. If it is the former, then you need to talk to that person per the teachings of Christ. If it is the latter, then sin is incurred. In short, we should cultivate charity within our own heart. Jesus warns us that the "measure you use against others will be the same measure that will be used on you" (Matthew 7:2). If we spent the time we waste on gossip, praying for the good of the person we gossip about, we would find ourselves in a much holier and peaceful place.

Now, please excuse me as I contemplate all possible meanings of "Physician heal thyself."

Prayer of Reparation

My Lord and my God, we have allowed the temptation of the devil to move our hearts against our brothers and sisters. We have gossiped about our brothers and sisters instead of seeking their conversion and good. We have allowed rash judgement to harden our hearts. We have expected You to be pleased with or blind to our sin. We have, at times, been a source of scandal for those searching through our sinfulness and rebellion to You. In our fear, we have allowed the ancient foe to advance. We turn to You Lord, in our sorrow and guilt, and beg Your forgiveness for our gossip in all its forms. We beg for the grace of Your goodness to build up within us what You sought to build up in Your apostles in that tempest-tossed boat. We know, Lord, if You will it, it will be done. Trusting in You, we offer our prayer to You who live and reign forever and ever. Amen

Prayer of Exorcism

Lord God of heaven and earth, in Your power and goodness, You created all things. You set a path for us to walk on and a way to an eternal relationship. By the strength of Your arm and Word of Your mouth, cast from Your Holy Church every fearful deceit of the devil. Drive from us manifestations of the demonic that oppress us and beckon us to gossip. Still the lying tongue of the devil and his forces so that we may act freely and faithfully to Your will. Send Your holy angels to cast out all influence that the demonic entities in charge of gossip, detraction, calumny, and rash judgement have planted in Your Church. Free us, our families, our parish, our diocese, and our country from all trickery and deceit perpetrated by the devil and his hellish legions. Trusting in Your goodness Lord, we know if You will it, it will be done, in unity with Your Son and the Holy Spirit, One God forever and ever. Amen.

⌂ DAY 37 CHECKLIST ⌂

__ Prayer for Freedom from the Devil - pg. 255

__ Daily reflection and prayers

__ Litany of the day – pg. 256

__ Pray a Rosary (intention: exorcism of gossip) – pg.275

__ Divine Mercy Chaplet (in reparation for: sin due to gossip) – pg. 279

__ Spiritual or corporal work of mercy (see pg. 254)

__ Fast/abstain (according to level)

__ Exercise (according to level/ability)

__ Refrain from conventional media (only 1 hr. of social)

__ Examination of conscience (confession 1x this week)

Day 38
Freedom from WORLDLINESS
By FR. RICHARD HEILMAN

This being the finale of my reflections for *Let Freedom Ring* (LFR), I felt called to write about the amazing "Life of Grace." Almost all those who have been participating in LFR have enlisted in the United States Grace Force. At this writing, the Grace Force is 76,000 strong. The Grace Force adheres to St. Paul's call to get strong: "Be strong in the Lord and in his mighty power. Put on the full armor of God, so that You can take Your stand against the devil's schemes" (Eph 6:10-11).

By choosing to live in God's supernatural grace, we are choosing a life lived beyond the low life of mere worldliness and, instead, we are choosing to live the "higher life" in God's grace, described so well by Archbishop Fulton Sheen:

> "Christ's reason for taking upon Himself a human nature was to pay for sin by death on the cross and to bring us a higher life ... This higher life which is divine, distinct from the human, is called grace, because it is *gratis* or a free gift of God ... Man may live at three different levels: the sensate, the intellectual, and the divine. These may be likened to a three-story house.
>
> The sensate level, or the first floor, represents those who deny any other reality except the pleasures that come from the flesh. Their

house is rather poorly furnished and is capable of giving intermittent thrills which quickly dry up. The occupant of this first floor is not interested in being told of higher levels of existence; in fact, he may even deny their existence.

On the second floor, there is the intellectual level of existence, that of the scientist, the historian, the journalist, the humanist; the man who has brought to a peak all of the powers of human reason and human will. This is a much more comfortable kind of existence, and far more satisfying to the human spirit. Those on the second floor may think their floor is 'a closed universe,' regarding as superstitious those who desire a higher form of life.

But there is actually a third floor which is the floor of grace by which the human heart is illumined by truths which reason cannot know; by which the will is strengthened by a power quite beyond all psychological aids, and the heart is entranced with the love which never fails; which gives a peace that cannot be found on the two lower levels ...

The world, therefore, is divided into the 'once born' and the 'twice born': between the sons of the old Adam, and the sons of the new Adam, Christ; between the unregenerate and the regenerate. There is a real inequality in the world. There are 'superior' and 'inferior' peoples, but the basis of distinction is not color, race, nationality, or wealth. The superior people of the earth are the supermen, the God-men; the inferior people are those who have been called to that superior state but, as yet, have not embraced it."

Boil everything down, and we see that this is at the heart of the battle today. While we are called to be "Supermen/God-men," the "influencers" of our culture are pulling us down to that base and brute level of existence. These influencers, known as the "ruling class" (elites), are actually the inferior people who dwell on the first two floors, who believe and

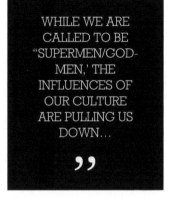

WHILE WE ARE CALLED TO BE "SUPERMEN/GOD-MEN,' THE INFLUENCES OF OUR CULTURE ARE PULLING US DOWN...

promote that we are nothing more than another animal species. As I pointed out in a previous reflection, the influencers are the media, Hollywood, TV, politicians, universities, public schools, etc., who relentlessly promote the false gods of sexual hedonism and radical narcissism. "If it feels good, just do it." This is the "law of animals."

Add to this, we are emerging from a very grim period of spiritual weakness where most Christians ceased to believe in the supernatural power of God. As a result, Satan and his minions have been able to move almost unabated while, in spiritual terms, we have stood naked on the battlefield with no spiritual armor and no spiritual weapons to combat Satan's evil designs. Thank God, we are witnessing a renaissance of "belief" in the supernatural power of God.

Under the power of supernatural grace, we are called to lift ourselves up, along with the entire world, into the "higher life" of the principals, morals, ethics, values, and virtues of God that raises every society out of darkness and chaos into the light of truth and peace. President Ronald Reagan once famously stated, "We maintain the peace through our strength; weakness only invites aggression." The Grace Force uses the motto, "Peace through Strength" (in Latin, *Per Virtutem Pax*). Spiritual warfare is about our resolve to become strong in God's supernatural power; the only power capable of "shining out" the dark and aggressive satanic forces of evil.

Go to Confession frequently. Go to Confession frequently. Go to Confession frequently. And walk humbly with your God. So, pray as though you believe God is right there listening; humbly obey "all" Church teachings; look for opportunities to, selflessly, be a light in others' lives; and BELIEVE in the power of God!

Be in the world, but not of the world. Be Supermen! (or, Superwomen!). Be Saints! Be-lieve!

Prayer of Reparation

My Lord and my God, we have allowed the temptation of the devil to move our hearts toward fearfully allowing the spread of worldliness throughout our culture and our Catholic Church. We have fallen into this widespread worldliness when we have not lived up to the call of our baptism to, day-by-day, deepen our love and faith in You. We have been too easily swayed by the poor example of worldliness, in churches everywhere, and have not encouraged a deeper sense of supernatural faith. In our weakness, we have allowed the ancient foe to advance. We turn to You Lord, in our sorrow and guilt, and beg Your forgiveness for any of our own worldliness or our lack of resolve to lift souls out of worldliness and into the High Life of grace. We beg for the grace of Your goodness to build up within us the strength and endurance to be this visible light of fervent faith in You. We know, Lord, if You will it, it will be done. Trusting in You, we offer our prayer to You who live and reign forever and ever. Amen.

Prayer of Exorcism

Lord God of heaven and earth, in Your power and goodness, You created all things. You set a path for us to walk on and a way to an eternal relationship. By the strength of Your arm and Word of Your mouth, cast from Your Holy Church every fearful deceit of the devil. Drive from us manifestations of the demonic that oppress us and beckon us to worldliness. Still the lying tongue of the devil and his forces so that we may act freely and faithfully to do Your will. Send Your holy angels to cast out all influence that the demonic entities in charge of worldliness have planted in Your Church. Free us, our families, our parish, our diocese, and our country from all trickery and deceit perpetrated by the devil and his hellish legions. Trusting in Your goodness Lord, we know if You will it, it will be done, in unity with Your Son and the Holy Spirit, One God forever and ever. Amen.

⌂DAY 38 CHECKLIST⌂

___ Prayer for Freedom from the Devil - pg. 255

___ Daily reflection and prayers

___ Litany of the day – pg. 256

___ Pray a Rosary (intention: exorcism of worldliness) – pg.275

___ Divine Mercy Chaplet (in reparation for: sin due to worldliness) – pg. 279

___ Spiritual or corporal work of mercy (see pg. 254)

___ Fast/abstain (according to level)

___ Exercise (according to level/ability)

___ Refrain from conventional media (only 1 hr. of social)

___ Examination of conscience (confession 1x this week)

Day 39
Freedom from PRESUMPTION
By FR. JAMES ALTMAN

Dear family, we are almost to the end of the forty days. What a holy, holy endeavor with so much grace, so very much grace. This grace we need now, more than ever, with all the crazy stuff going on around us. The best words to wrap up my part are words of encouragement. Keep going. Do not stop now, for we are not yet at the end of our time on earth. Rather, Our Father has chosen us to live in this time and place, and to serve Him in this time and in this place. What we have endured, amidst the abandonment of so many shepherds, is only a precursor to what may be coming soon. The spiritually weakened state of so many out there will not bode well when worse things come. To me, this entire holy endeavor was a spiritual boot camp to toughen us up, to make us strong enough to fight the battles that lie ahead.

> OUR FATHER HAS CHOSEN US TO LIVE IN THIS TIME AND PLACE, AND TO SERVE HIM IN THIS TIME AND IN THIS PLACE.
>
> **"**

Fr. Heilman tells me that thousands will join us in this spiritual boot camp. That is amazing. It tells us, dear family, that we are not alone. But maybe the number should be hundreds of thousands. In fact, the grotesque abandonment by so many shepherds is even more reason why there should be millions. So, why aren't there that many, and more? A big reason, probably the biggest reason, is the sin of presumption.

As always, a good starting place is Fr. John Hardon's *Modern Catholic Dictionary*. He states that presumption "leads one to expect graces from God without doing anything to obtain them, and even when acting the opposite, as when sinning, the person presumes that forgiveness is assured." (etymology: Latin *"praesumere"*, to suppose, take for granted.) Donald Attwater's, *A Catholic Dictionary* writes similarly that presumption is "a vice … whereby a man expects to gain eternal life by his own strength or without merits, or to obtain pardon without repentance."

Wow. There it is in a nutshell. I don't have to reinvent the wheel; that is the beauty of being Catholic. We have 2000 years of the Bible, 2000 years of saints and martyrs, 2000 years of the constant teaching of the Catholic Church, 2000 years of the unchanged and unchangeable truth. So, unlike, say, Joel Osteen et al. who wallow in presumption, we know that as a disciple of Jesus the Lord, we are charged to pick up our crosses daily and carry them. We must not carry them for five minutes and set them down; that's not what Jesus said. Jesus did not say, "clock in, carry for 8 hours, clock out." Jesus did not say, "any time after eight hours is overtime, time-and-a-half." No. The real Jesus said, in essence, "take it from Me when you wake up, let Me hold it close while you sleep."

Our crosses mean that we must make an effort to grow in grace daily. Truly, we can never be worthy of the salvation for which Jesus endured His Passion, and thankfully, He does not ask us to be. He asks us only to pick up our crosses daily. Yet so many do not. Presumption is bad enough amongst Catholics, but in so many Protestants it is even worse. That whole "I just asked JAY-zus into my heart and I'm SAAAAVED" is so much presumption baloney. Jesus never said that. Jesus said to pick up your cross...daily.

Amongst Catholics, there seems to be way too many with a similar attitude – an attitude that has become pervasive since we have been inculcated with all the meaningless drivel put out after Vatican II. One that thinks, "Oh, Our Father loves us all and doesn't want anybody to go to hell, so since I didn't do something really bad, like kill somebody, I'm good to go." Or one that hopes, as a well-known shepherd recently posited, that hell is actually kind of an empty place. Really? That is not what Jesus taught about hell. The presumptuous mindset of "I'm good enough" is not the standard Jesus set on Calvary.

Cardinal St. John Henry Newman brilliantly eviscerated the attitude of presumption when he observed "that [the aim of most men] is, to all appearances, not how to please God, but how to please themselves without displeasing Him!"

Jesus spoke specifically to such an attitude in a parable that addressed those who were convinced of their own righteousness. Remember the Pharisee "took up his position [in the Temple] and spoke this prayer to himself, 'O God, I thank You that I am not like the rest of humanity—greedy, dishonest, adulterous—or even like this tax collector." Jesus then contrasted that attitude with the sinner who "stood off at a distance and would not even raise his eyes to heaven but beat his breast and prayed, 'O God, be merciful to me a sinner." Jesus then said: "I tell you, the latter went home justified, not the former; for everyone who exalts himself will be humbled, and the one who humbles himself will be exalted" (Luke 18:9-14). So, dear family, let us be incredibly careful about justifying our own righteousness, and exalting our status vis-à-vis our eternal destination.

Instead of being self-righteous, Jesus gave another parable about the right attitude of one of His disciples, or servants, "Is [God] grateful to that servant because he did what was commanded? … When You have done all You have been commanded, say, 'We are unprofitable servants; we have done [only] what we were obliged to do'" (Luke 17:9-10).

Dear family, let us conclude with a sports analogy. There is no "I" in team. That's why the Protestant attitude about "me 'n JAY-zus" is just pure garbage. Jesus is a team effort. He calls us to be part of His team. That means that every day is another day for each team member to show up for practice – practice to be a better team player. Each person on the team has a position to play, and the better that person plays, the better the team (which is why, by the way, that blowing off attendance at Holy Mass on Sunday is not just a grave personal sin but is a grave sin against the whole team). What happens when a player doesn't show up for practice? At best, he "rides the pine" (meaning, he sits on the bench). The coach – in this case, God – cannot give him playing time, because he hasn't practiced. He has let the whole team down. That is what happens at best. At worst, he gets kicked off the team (welcome to hell).

Dear family, here is one last way to understand the sin of presumption. Again, think of it as an attitude of "good enough." There is a quote, with many variations, all of which say the same thing: "The attitude of 'good enough' is the enemy of 'great.'" Put another way, "the enemy of 'great' is not 'bad', the enemy of 'great' is 'good enough.'"

Our Father offered up the Greatest on Calvary. Does our offering – through the carrying of our crosses – measure up to such greatness?

The cure for the sin of presumption is to strive daily to not do JUST what we have been commanded to do. That only makes us a useless servant. The cure for the sin of presumption is to do MORE than we have been commanded to do.

So, now that we are reaching the end of our forty days of preparation, let us do more. Let us continue to practice daily with the U.S. Grace Force Team (join at usgraceforce.com). Let us continue to make the Catholic Team strong, with all of us earning our playing time in the game.

Prayer of Reparation

My Lord and my God, we have allowed the temptation of the devil to move our hearts toward presumption. We think we are good enough. We can recognize our attitude of presumption whenever we simply do not show up for practice – whenever we do not make the effort to spend an hour a day with You. At times we justify our presumption because we have so many other things we "need" to do. We ignore the plain truth that "if Satan can't make You bad, he will make You busy." At times we do not recognize in ourselves that we are the Pharisee who said, "thank God I'm not like all those sinners back there." Too infrequently do we approach the Sacrament of Confession of sins. Too infrequently do we examine our conscience and see we really are sinners. Too infrequently do we say to ourselves that we are unprofitable servants; for we have done only what we were obliged to do. So often we just do not recognize our presumption. We turn to You Lord, in our weakness, and beg Your forgiveness for our presumption, and especially for all the times we have failed to practice with and for Your team, for all the times we have let down our teammates. We love You, Lord, and we beg for the wisdom and strength to love You more. We know Lord, if You will it, it will be done. Trusting in You, we offer our prayer to You who live and reign forever and ever. Amen.

Prayer of Exorcism

Lord God of heaven and earth, in Your power and goodness, You created all things. You set a path for us to walk on and a way to an eternal relationship. By the strength of Your arm and Word of Your mouth, cast from Your Holy Church every fearful deceit of the devil. Drive from us manifestations of the demonic that oppress us and beckon us to presumption. Still the lying tongue of the devil and his forces so that we may act freely and faithfully to Your will. Send Your holy angels to cast out all influence that the demonic entities in charge of presumption have planted in Your Church. Free us, our families, our parish, our diocese, and our country from all trickery and deceit perpetrated by the devil and his hellish legions. Trusting in Your goodness Lord, we know if You will it, it will be done, in unity with Your Son and the Holy Spirit, one God, forever and ever. Amen.

🔔 DAY 39 CHECKLIST 🔔

__ Prayer for Freedom from the Devil - pg. 255

__ Daily reflection and prayers

__ Litany of the day – pg. 256

__ Pray a Rosary (intention: exorcism of presumption) – pg.275

__ Divine Mercy Chaplet (in reparation for: sin due to presumption) – pg. 279

__ Spiritual or corporal work of mercy (see pg. 254)

__ Fast/abstain (according to level)

__ Exercise (according to level/ability)

__ Refrain from conventional media (only 1 hr. of social)

__ Examination of conscience (confession 1x this week)

Day 40
Freedom from SLOTH
By FR. WILLIAM PECKMAN

Here we are at the end of 40 days of prayer, fasting, and abstinence, asking for God to purge all demonic influences from our lives and lives of the Church. If we have been faithful to the program of prayer and fasting/abstinence, we should have begun a new way of life where we can incorporate such things into our daily routines. Forty days is hardly sufficient to cast all diabolic activity from our lives, our society, and within our Church. What we hope to do is start new and better habits.

Fr. Heilman wrote a wonderful column on acedia, the slothfulness we often display to spiritual matters. Certainly, we will experience temptation to backtrack on our renewed spiritual vigor. As I tell my parishioners at the beginning of Lent, "the point of the next 40 days isn't to make yourself uncomfortable and miserable for the sake of making yourself uncomfortable and miserable." Instead, we have committed ourselves to detachment from the diabolical, much the same way an excellent athlete commits to a workout regimen, or the way a scholar commits to their academics. The goal is to become stronger, and through prayer and fasting, holier.

However, sloth can be a sneaky demonic presence. It is an unwillingness to exert effort or to work. Sloth sees comfort as an end goal, so it leads us to steal time and energy from our jobs, families, and faith in the interest of self. It can lead us to procrastination and half-heartedly attending to the duties that others count on us doing.

The failure to challenge oneself, or to completely abandon one's responsibilities, has spiritual effects that I often liken to its physical and intellectual counterparts. For

example, if we are slothful on the physical front, it leads to poor health, loss of muscle mass, and obesity. The body must be taken care of. It must be correctly fed and exercised to stay strong and healthy. Sloth in the physical realm can have a grave cost. If we are slothful in the intellectual realm, not only do we not grow smarter, but we also lose knowledge that we had prior gained. This can have devastating consequences on a person who is in school (ex. grades) or in the workplace. Sloth eats away at any strength or success that might be gained in the physical or intellectual realms. As remarked in the column of acedia, sloth in the spiritual realm leads to a denigration of the spiritual life and breaks down, and distances us in, our relationship with God. Sloth is ultimately another form of selfishness.

To fight this deadly sin, we must look to the cardinal virtue of justice. Justice helps us to assume our responsibilities and to give to others what is rightfully due. Justice leads us away from a slavish devotion to comfort and provokes us to use our God-given abilities and talents for a greater good. It encourages us to treat those tools God has blessed us with (body, mind, and soul) in such a way as to be able to fulfill our purpose. It helps us take care of all aspects of ourselves. Justice helps us be wise and steadfast stewards of God's gifts in our lives, and to be diligent in the duties and relationships we are called to live in. The purpose of our exercise in prayer, fasting, and abstinence has been to detach ourselves from worldly comfort, looking to another and higher goal.

At the end of these 40 days, let us remember the motto of Bl. Pier Giorgio Frasatti, *"verso l'alto"* (to the heights), and let the good habits we have engaged in lead us to a greater holiness and life in Christ.

Prayer of Reparation

My Lord and my God, we have allowed the temptation of the devil to move our hearts to sloth, laziness, and disordered love of ease. We have allowed ourselves to be negligent and unjust to those around us. We have allowed ourselves to squander the great gifts You have given us of our minds, bodies, and souls. We have expected You to turn a blind eye to our sloth and reward our lack of justice. We have, at times, been a source of scandal for those searching through our sinfulness and rebellion to You. In our fear, we have allowed the ancient foe to advance. We turn to You Lord, in our sorrow and guilt, and beg Your forgiveness for sloth in all its forms. We beg for the grace of Your goodness to build up within us what You sought to build up in Your apostles in that tempest-tossed boat.

We know Lord, if You will it, it will be done. Trusting in You, we offer our prayer to You who live and reign forever. Amen.

Prayer of Exorcism

Lord God of heaven and earth, in Your power and goodness, You created all things. You set a path for us to walk on and a way to an eternal relationship. By the strength of Your arm and Word of Your mouth, cast from Your Holy Church every fearful deceit of the devil. Drive from us manifestations of the demonic that oppress us and beckon us to sloth. Still the lying tongue of the devil and his forces so that we may act freely and faithfully to Your will. Send Your holy angels to cast out all influence that the demonic entities in charge of sloth have planted in Your Church. Free us, our families, our parish, our diocese, and our country from all trickery and deceit perpetrated by the devil and his hellish legions. Trusting in Your goodness Lord, we know if You will it, it will be done, in unity with Your Son and the Holy Spirit, One God forever and ever. Amen.

♤ DAY 40 CHECKLIST ♤

___ Prayer for Freedom from the Devil - pg. 255

___ Daily reflection and prayers

___ Litany of the day – pg. 256

___ Pray a Rosary (intention: exorcism of sloth) – pg.275

___ Divine Mercy Chaplet (in reparation for: sin due to sloth) – pg. 279

___ Spiritual or corporal work of mercy (see pg. 254)

___ Fast/abstain (according to level)

___ Exercise (according to level/ability)

___ Refrain from conventional media (only 1 hr. of social)

___ Examination of conscience (confession 1x this week)

ACKNOWLEDGMENTS

We three priests are eternally grateful to all whose work helped to write this book, including: Joe Balistreri, Trese Gloriod, Zip Rzeppa, Emily Seyfert, and Kari Sherman.

We would also like to acknowledge all our family, friends, and mentors, living and deceased, whose teaching and example helped clear the pathway to God.

Finally, we know and feel the many prayers of all the saints in the making on earth and all the saints in heaven. Thank you!

Appendix A

Works of Mercy and Prayer for Freedom from the Devil

Spiritual Works of Mercy

1. Instruct the Ignorant
2. Counsel the Doubtful
3. Admonish the Sinners
4. Forgive Offenses
5. Comfort the Afflicted
6. Bear Wrongs Patiently
7. Pray for the Living and the Dead

Corporal Works of Mercy

1. Feed the Hungry
2. Give Drink to the Thirsty
3. Shelter the Homeless
4. Clothe the Naked
5. Visit the Sick
6. Visit the Imprisoned
7. Bury the Dead

Prayer for Freedom from the Devil

(Begin with this prayer each day)

My Lord and Savior Jesus Christ, at a word from You the devil and his minions flee in terror. You are the source of all truth. You are the source of all strength.

By the power of Your Cross and Resurrection, we beseech You, O Lord, to extend Your saving arm and to send Your holy angels to defend us as we do battle with Satan and his demonic forces.

Exorcise, we pray, that which oppresses Your Bride, the Church, so that within ourselves, our families, our parishes, our dioceses, and our nation we may turn fully back to You in all fidelity and trust.

Lord, we know if You will it, it will be done. Give us the perseverance for this mission, we pray. Amen.

Our Lady of the Immaculate Conception, pray for us.

St. Joseph, pray for us.

St. Michael the Archangel, pray for us.

(The patron of your parish), pray for us.

(Your confirmation saint), pray for us.

Appendix B
Litanies

Litany of Humility (on Mondays)

O Jesus, meek and humble of heart, Hear me.

From the desire of being esteemed,
> Deliver me, O Jesus.

From the desire of being loved,
> Deliver me, O Jesus.

From the desire of being extolled,
> Deliver me, O Jesus.

From the desire of being honored,
> Deliver me, O Jesus.

From the desire of being praised,
> Deliver me, O Jesus.

From the desire of being preferred to others,
> Deliver me, O Jesus.

From the desire of being consulted,
> Deliver me, O Jesus.

From the desire of being approved,
> Deliver me, O Jesus.

From the fear of being humiliated,
> Deliver me, O Jesus.

From the fear of being despised,
> Deliver me, O Jesus.

From the fear of suffering rebukes,
> Deliver me, O Jesus.

From the fear of being calumniated,

    Deliver me, O Jesus.

From the fear of being forgotten,

    Deliver me, O Jesus.

From the fear of being ridiculed,

    Deliver me, O Jesus.

From the fear of being wronged,

    Deliver me, O Jesus.

From the fear of being suspected,

    Deliver me, O Jesus.

That others may be loved more than I,

    Jesus, grant me the grace to desire it.

That others may be esteemed more than I,

    Jesus, grant me the grace to desire it.

That, in the opinion of the world, others may
increase and I may decrease,

    Jesus, grant me the grace to desire it.

That others may be chosen and I set aside,

    Jesus, grant me the grace to desire it.

That others may be praised and I go unnoticed,

    Jesus, grant me the grace to desire it.

That others may be preferred to me in everything,

    Jesus, grant me the grace to desire it.

That others may become holier than I, provided that
I may become as holy as I should,

    Jesus, grant me the grace to desire it.

Litany of St. Michael the Archangel
(on Tuesdays)

Lord, have mercy on us.

Christ, have mercy on us.

Lord, have mercy on us.

Christ, hear us.

Christ, graciously hear us.

God the Father of Heaven, have mercy on us.

God the Son, Redeemer of the world,
   have mercy on us.

God the Holy Ghost, have mercy on us.

Holy Trinity, one God, have mercy on us.

Holy Mary, Queen of the Angels, pray for us.

St. Michael, the Archangel, pray for us.

Most glorious attendant of the Triune Divinity,
   pray for us.

Standing at the right of the altar of Incense,
   pray for us.

Ambassador of Paradise, pray for us.

Glorious Prince of the Heavenly armies, pray for us.

Leader of the Angelic hosts, pray for us.

The standard-bearer of God's armies, pray for us.

Defender of Divine glory, pray for us.

First defender of the Kingship of Christ, pray for us.

Strength of God, pray for us.

Invincible Prince and warrior, pray for us.

Angel of Peace, pray for us.

Guide of Christ, pray for us.

Guardian of the Catholic Faith, pray for us.

Champion of God's people, pray for us.

Guardian Angel of the Eucharist, pray for us.

Defender of the Church, pray for us.

Protector of the Sovereign Pontiff, pray for us.

Angel of Catholic action, pray for us.

Powerful intercessor of Christians, pray for us.

Bravest defender of those who hope in God,
pray for us.

Guardian of our souls and bodies, pray for us.

Healer of the sick, pray for us.

Help of those in their agony, pray for us.

Consoler of the Souls in Purgatory, pray for us.

God's messenger for the souls of the just,
pray for us.

Terror of the evil spirits, pray for us.

Victorious in battle against evil, pray for us.

Guardian and Patron of the universal Church,
pray for us.

Lamb of God, Who takest away the sins of the
world, spare us, O Lord.

Lamb of God, Who takest away the sins of the
world, graciously hear us, O Lord.

Lamb of God, Who takest away the sins of the
world, have mercy on us.

V. Pray for us, O glorious St. Michael,

R. That we may be made worthy of the promises of
Christ.

Let us pray.

Relying, O Lord, upon the intercession of Thy blessed archangel Michael, we humbly beg of Thee, that the Sacrament of the Eucharist which we have received may make our souls holy and pleasing to Thee. Through Christ our Lord. Amen.

Litany of St. Joseph (on Wednesdays)

Lord, have mercy on us.

Christ, have mercy on us.

Lord, have mercy on us.

Christ, hear us.

Christ, graciously hear us.

God the Father of Heaven, Have mercy on us.

God the Son, Redeemer of the world, Have mercy on us.

God the Holy Spirit, Have mercy on us.

Holy Trinity, One God, Have mercy on us.

Holy Mary, pray for us.

Saint Joseph, pray for us.

Illustrious son of David, pray for us.

Light of the patriarchs, pray for us.

Spouse of the Mother of God, pray for us.

Chaste guardian of the Virgin, pray for us.

Foster-father of the Son of God, pray for us.

Watchful defender of Christ, pray for us.

Head of the Holy Family, pray for us.

Joseph most just, pray for us.

Joseph most chaste, pray for us.

Joseph most prudent, pray for us.

Joseph most valiant, pray for us.

Joseph most obedient, pray for us.

Joseph most faithful, pray for us.

Mirror of patience, pray for us.

Lover of poverty, pray for us.

Model of workmen, pray for us.

Glory of domestic life, pray for us.

Guardian of virgins, pray for us.

Pillar of families, pray for us.

Solace of the afflicted, pray for us.

Hope of the sick, pray for us.

Patron of the dying, pray for us.

Terror of demons, pray for us.

Protector of Holy Church, pray for us.

Lamb of God, Who takest away the sins of the
world, Spare us, O Lord.

Lamb of God, Who takest away the sins of the
world, Graciously hear us, O Lord.

Lamb of God, Who takest away the sins of the
world, Have mercy on us.

V. He made him the lord of His household,

R. And prince over all His possessions.

Let us pray:

O God, Who in Thine ineffable providence didst
choose Blessed Joseph to be the spouse of Thy
most Holy Mother, grant that as we venerate him

as our protector on earth, we may deserve to have him as our intercessor in Heaven, Thou Who livest and reignest forever and ever.

R. Amen.

Litany of the Most Precious Blood of Jesus
(on Thursdays)

Lord, have mercy on us.

Christ, have mercy on us.

Lord, have mercy on us.

Christ, hear us.

Christ, graciously hear us.

God, the Father of Heaven, have mercy on us.

God the Son, Redeemer of the world, have mercy on us.

God, the Holy Spirit, have mercy on us.

Holy Trinity, One God, have mercy on us.

Blood of Christ, only-begotten Son of the Eternal Father, save us.

Blood of Christ, Incarnate Word of God, save us.

Blood of Christ, of the New and Eternal Testament, save us.

Blood of Christ, falling upon the earth in the Agony, save us.

Blood of Christ, shed profusely in the Scourging, save us.

Blood of Christ, flowing forth in the Crowning with Thorns, save us.

Blood of Christ, poured out on the Cross, save us.

Blood of Christ, price of our salvation, save us.

Blood of Christ, without which there is no
forgiveness, save us.

Blood of Christ, Eucharistic drink and refreshment
of souls, save us.

Blood of Christ, stream of mercy, save us.

Blood of Christ, victor over demons, save us.

Blood of Christ, courage of martyrs, save us.

Blood of Christ, strength of confessors, save us.

Blood of Christ, bringing forth virgins, save us.

Blood of Christ, help of those in peril, save us.

Blood of Christ, relief of the burdened, save us.

Blood of Christ, solace in sorrow, save us.

Blood of Christ, hope of the penitent, save us.

Blood of Christ, consolation of the dying, save us.

Blood of Christ, peace and tenderness of hearts,
save us.

Blood of Christ, pledge of Eternal Life, save us.

Blood of Christ, freeing souls from purgatory,
save us.

Blood of Christ, most worthy of all glory and honor,
save us.

Lamb of God, Who takest away the sins of the
world, Spare us, O Lord.

Lamb of God, Who takest away the sins of the
world, Graciously hear us, O Lord.

Lamb of God, Who takest away the sins of the
world, Have mercy on us.

V. Thou hast redeemed us, O Lord, in Thy Blood.

R. And made us, for our God, a kingdom.

Let us pray:

Almighty and eternal God, Thou hast appointed
Thine only-begotten Son the Redeemer of the
world and willed to be appeased by His blood.
Grant, we beg of Thee, that we may worthily
adore this price of our salvation and through its
power be safeguarded from the evils of the
present life so that we may rejoice in its fruits
forever in heaven. Through the same Christ our
Lord. Amen.

Litany of the Sacred Heart of Jesus
(on Fridays)

Lord, have mercy on us.

Christ, have mercy on us.

Lord, have mercy on us.

Christ, hear us.

Christ graciously hear us

God the Father of Heaven, have mercy on us.

God the Son, Redeemer of the world, have mercy
on us.

God the Holy Spirit, have mercy on us.

Holy Trinity, One God, have mercy on us.

Heart of Jesus, Son of the Eternal Father,
have mercy on us.

Heart of Jesus, formed in the womb of the Virgin
Mother by the Holy Ghost, have mercy on us.

Heart of Jesus, united substantially with the word of
God, have mercy on us.

Heart of Jesus, of infinite majesty,
have mercy on us.

Heart of Jesus, holy temple of God,
have mercy on us.

Heart of Jesus, tabernacle of the Most High,
have mercy on us.

Heart of Jesus, house of God and gate of heaven,
have mercy on us.

Heart of Jesus, glowing furnace of charity,
have mercy on us.

Heart of Jesus, vessel of justice and love,
have mercy on us.

Heart of Jesus, full of goodness and love,
have mercy on us.

Heart of Jesus, abyss of all virtues,
have mercy on us.

Heart of Jesus, most worthy of all praise,
have mercy on us.

Heart of Jesus, king and center of all hearts,
have mercy on us.

Heart of Jesus, in whom are all the treasures of
wisdom and knowledge,
have mercy on us.

Heart of Jesus, in whom dwelleth all the fullness of
the Divinity,
have mercy on us.

Heart of Jesus, in whom the Father is well pleased,
  have mercy on us.
Heart of Jesus, we have all received,
  have mercy on us.
Heart of Jesus, desire of the everlasting hills,
  have mercy on us.
Heart of Jesus, patient and rich in mercy,
  have mercy on us.
Heart of Jesus, rich to all who invoke Thee,
  have mercy on us.
Heart of Jesus, fount of life and holiness,
  have mercy on us.
Heart of Jesus, propitiation for our sins,
  have mercy on us.
Heart of Jesus, saturated with revilings,
  have mercy on us.
Heart of Jesus, crushed for our iniquities,
  have mercy on us.
Heart of Jesus, made obedient unto death,
  have mercy on us.
Heart of Jesus, pierced with a lance,
  have mercy on us.
Heart of Jesus, source of all consolation,
  have mercy on us.
Heart of Jesus, our life and resurrection,
  have mercy on us.
Heart of Jesus, our peace and reconciliation,
  have mercy on us.

Heart of Jesus, victim for our sins,
    have mercy on us.
Heart of Jesus, salvation of those who hope in Thee,
    have mercy on us.
Heart of Jesus, hope of those who die in Thee,
    have mercy on us.
Heart of Jesus, delight of all saints,
    have mercy on us.
Lamb of God, Who takest away the sins of the
    world, Spare us, O Lord.
Lamb of God, Who takest away the sins of the
    world, Graciously hear us, O Lord.
Lamb of God Who takest away the sins of the world,
    Have mercy on us.
V. Jesus, meek and humble of Heart.
R. Make our hearts like unto Thine.
Let us pray:
Almighty and everlasting God, look upon the Heart
    of Thy well-beloved Son and upon the acts of
    praise and satisfaction which He renders unto
    Thee in the name of sinners; and do Thou, in
    Thy great goodness, grant pardon to them who
    seek Thy mercy, in the name of the same Son,
    Jesus Christ, who liveth and reigneth with Thee,
    world without end. Amen.

Litany of the Immaculate Heart of Mary
(on Saturdays)

Lord, have mercy on us.

Christ, have mercy on us.

Lord, have mercy on us.

Christ, hear us.

Christ, graciously hear us.

God the Father of Heaven, Have mercy on us.

God the Son, Redeemer of the world,

Have mercy on us.

God the Holy Ghost, Have mercy on us.

Holy Trinity, One God, Have mercy on us.

Heart of Mary, Pray for us.

Heart of Mary, like unto the Heart of God,

Pray for us.

Heart of Mary, united to the Heart of Jesus,

Pray for us.

Heart of Mary, instrument of the Holy Ghost,

Pray for us.

Heart of Mary, sanctuary of the Divine Trinity,

Pray for us.

Heart of Mary, tabernacle of God Incarnate,

Pray for us.

Heart of Mary, immaculate from thy creation,

Pray for us.

Heart of Mary, full of grace, Pray for us.

Heart of Mary, blessed among all hearts, Pray for us.

Heart of Mary, throne of glory, Pray for us.

Heart of Mary, most humble, Pray for us.

Heart of Mary, holocaust of Divine Love, Pray for us.

Heart of Mary, fastened to the Cross with Jesus Crucified, Pray for us.

Heart of Mary, comfort of the afflicted, Pray for us.

Heart of Mary, refuge of sinners, Pray for us.

Heart of Mary, hope of the agonizing, Pray for us.

Heart of Mary, seat of mercy, Pray for us.

Lamb of God, Who takest away the sins of the world, Spare us, O Lord.

Lamb of God, Who takest away the sins of the world, Graciously hear us, O Lord.

Lamb of God, Who takest away the sins of the world, Have mercy on us.

V. Immaculate Mary, meek and humble of heart,

R. Make our hearts like unto the Heart of Jesus.

Let us pray:

O most merciful God, Who, for the salvation of sinners and the refuge of the miserable, was pleased that the most pure heart of Mary should be most like in charity and pity to the Divine Heart of Thy Son, Jesus Christ, grant that we, who commemorate this sweet and loving heart, by the merits and intercession of the same Blessed Virgin, may merit to be found like unto the Heart of Jesus, through the same Christ Our Lord. Amen.

Litany of the Most Blessed Sacrament
(on Sundays)

Lord, have mercy on us.

Christ, have mercy on us.

Lord, have mercy on us.

Christ, hear us.

Christ, graciously hear us.

God the Father of Heaven, Have mercy on us.

God the Son, Redeemer of the world, Have mercy on us.

God the Holy Spirit, Have mercy on us.

Holy Trinity, one God, Have mercy on us.

Jesus, Eternal High Priest of the Eucharistic Sacrifice, have mercy on us.

Jesus, Divine Victim on the Altar for our salvation, have mercy on us.

Jesus, hidden under the appearance of bread, have mercy on us.

Jesus, dwelling in the tabernacles of the world, have mercy on us.

Jesus, really, truly and substantially present in the Blessed Sacrament, have mercy on us.

Jesus, abiding in Your fulness, Body, Blood, Soul and Divinity, have mercy on us.

Jesus, Bread of Life, have mercy on us.

Jesus, Bread of Angels, have mercy on us.

Jesus, with us always until the end of the world, have mercy on us.

Sacred Host, summit and source of all worship and
Christian life, have mercy on us.

Sacred Host, sign and cause of the unity of the
Church, have mercy on us.

Sacred Host, adored by countless angels,
have mercy on us.

Sacred Host, spiritual food, have mercy on us.

Sacred Host, Sacrament of love, have mercy on us.

Sacred Host, bond of charity, have mercy on us.

Sacred Host, greatest aid to holiness,
have mercy on us.

Sacred Host, gift and glory of the priesthood,
have mercy on us.

Sacred Host, in which we partake of Christ,
have mercy on us.

Sacred Host, in which the soul is filled with grace,
have mercy on us.

Sacred Host, in which we are given a pledge of future
glory, have mercy on us.

Blessed be Jesus in the Most Holy Sacrament of the
Altar.

Blessed be Jesus in the Most Holy Sacrament of the
Altar.

Blessed be Jesus in the Most Holy Sacrament of the
Altar.

For those who do not believe in Your Eucharistic
presence, have mercy, O Lord.

For those who are indifferent to the Sacrament of
Your love, have mercy on us.

For those who have offended You in the Holy
	Sacrament of the Altar, have mercy on us.
That we may show fitting reverence when entering
	Your holy temple, we beseech You, hear us.
That we may make suitable preparation before
	approaching the Altar, we beseech You, hear us.
That we may receive You frequently in Holy
	Communion with real devotion and true humility,
	we beseech You, hear us.
That we may never neglect to thank You for so
	wonderful a blessing, we beseech You, hear us.
That we may cherish time spent in silent prayer
	before You, we beseech You, hear us.
That we may grow in knowledge of this Sacrament
	of sacraments, we beseech You, hear us.
That all priests may have a profound love of the Holy
	Eucharist, we beseech You, hear us.
That they may celebrate the Holy Sacrifice of the
	Mass in accordance with its sublime dignity, we
	beseech You, hear us.
That we may be comforted and sanctified with Holy
	Viaticum at the hour of our death, we beseech
	You, hear us.
That we may see You one day face to face in Heaven,
	we beseech You, hear us.
Lamb of God, Who takest away the sins of the
	world, Spare us, O Lord.
Lamb of God, Who takest away the sins of the
	world, Graciously hear us, O Lord.

Lamb of God, Who takest away the sins of the world, Have mercy on us.

V. O Sacrament Most Holy, O Sacrament Divine,

R. All praise and all thanksgiving be every moment Thine.

Let us pray:

Most merciful Father, You continue to draw us to Yourself through the Eucharistic Mystery. Grant us fervent faith in this sacrament of love, in which Christ the Lord Himself is contained, offered, and received. We make this prayer through the same Christ, our Lord. Amen.

Appendix C
Devotions

The Holy Rosary

How to Pray the Rosary

1. While holding the crucifix, make the **Sign of the Cross** and say the **Apostles Creed.**
2. Move to the first bead and pray the **Our Father.**
3. On each of the next 3 beads pray a **Hail Mary**
4. In the space after the 3 beads pray the **Glory Be.**
5. On the next larger bead announce the first mystery for the day and pray an **Our Father**.
6. Skip over the center medallion to the next smaller bead. On each of these 10 beads pray a **Hail Mary** while meditating on the first mystery.
7. In the space after the 10ᵗʰ small bead pray a **Glory Be** followed by the **Fatima Prayer**.
8. Repeat steps 5-7 for the next four sections of one larger bead followed by 10 smaller ones. Each of these sections is known as a "decade" and you should announce and meditate on the second, third, fourth, and fifth mysteries, respectively.
9. On the large center medallion say the **Hail, Holy Queen** followed by the **Closing Prayers** and the **Sign of the Cross**.

Mysteries of the Rosary

Joyful Mysteries (Mondays & Saturdays)
1. The Annunciation
2. The Visitation
3. The Nativity
4. The Presentation
5. The Finding of Jesus in the Temple

Sorrowful Mysteries (Tuesdays & Fridays)
1. The Agony in the Garden
2. The Scourging at the Pillar
3. The Crowning with Thorns
4. The Carrying of the Cross
5. The Crucifixion

Glorious Mysteries (Sundays & Wednesdays)
1. The Resurrection
2. The Ascension
3. The Descent of the Holy Spirit
4. The Assumption
5. The Coronation of Our Lady

Luminous Mysteries (On Thursdays)
1. The Baptism of Christ in the Jordan
2. The Wedding at Cana
3. The Proclamation of the Kingdom of God
4. The Transfiguration
5. The Institution of the Eucharist

Notes
* During the season of Advent, the Joyful Mysteries are also prayed on Sundays.

* During the season of Lent, the Sorrowful Mysteries are also prayed on Sundays.

Prayers of the Rosary

Sign of the Cross

In the name of the Father, and of the Son, and of the Holy Spirit. Amen.

The Apostles Creed

I believe in God, the Father Almighty, Creator of heaven and earth, and in Jesus Christ, His only Son, our Lord, who was conceived by the Holy Spirit, born of the Virgin Mary, suffered under Pontius Pilate, was crucified, died and was buried; He descended into hell; on the third day He rose again from the dead; He ascended into heaven, and is seated at the right hand of God the Father Almighty; from there He will come to judge the living and the dead. I believe in the Holy Spirit, the Holy Catholic Church, the communion of Saints, the forgiveness of sins, the resurrection of the body, and life everlasting. Amen.

Our Father

Our Father who art in heaven, hallowed be Thy name; Thy kingdom come; Thy will be done on earth as it is in heaven. Give us this day our daily bread; and forgive us our trespasses as we forgive those who trespass against us. And lead us not into temptation; but deliver us from evil. Amen.

Hail Mary

Hail, Mary, full of grace, the Lord is with thee. Blessed art thou among women, and blessed is the fruit of thy womb, Jesus. Holy Mary, Mother of God, pray for us sinners, now and at the hour of our death. Amen.

Glory Be

Glory be to the Father, and to the Son, and to the Holy Spirit, as it was in the beginning, is now, and ever shall be, world without end. Amen.

Fatima Prayer

O my Jesus, forgive us our sins, save us from the fires of hell. Lead all souls to heaven, especially those most in need of thy mercy. Amen.

Hail, Holy Queen

Hail, Holy Queen, Mother of Mercy, our life, our sweetness, and our hope. To thee do we cry, poor banished children of Eve; to thee do we send up our sighs, mourning and weeping in this valley of tears. Turn, then, most gracious advocate, thine eyes of mercy toward us, and after this, our exile, show unto us the blessed fruit of thy womb, Jesus.

V. O clement, O loving, O sweet Virgin Mary.

R. Pray for us, O Holy Mother of God, that we may be made worthy of the promises of Christ.

Closing Prayer

O God, whose only begotten Son, by His life, death, and resurrection has purchased for us the rewards of eternal life, grant we beseech Thee, that meditating upon these mysteries of the Most Holy Rosary of the Blessed Virgin Mary, we may imitate what they contain and obtain what they promise, through the same Christ our Lord. Amen.

The Divine Mercy Chaplet

How to pray the Divine Mercy Chaplet

1. On the crucifix, make the **Sign of the Cross.**
2. On the first bead say the optional **Opening Prayers.**
3. On the first smaller bead say the **Our Father.**
4. On the second smaller bead say the **Hail Mary**
5. On the third smaller bead say the **Apostles Creed.**
6. On the next larger bead say the **Eternal Father**
7. Jump over the medallion; for each of the 10 smaller beads in the decade say the **For the Sake of His Sorrowful Passion** prayer.
8. Repeat steps 6 and 7 for the remaining four decades.
9. On the center medallion repeat the **Concluding Doxology** three times, and then say the optional **Closing Prayer**

Prayers for the Divine Mercy Chaplet

Sign of the Cross

In the name of the Father, and of the Son, and of the Holy
Spirit. Amen.

Opening Prayers

You expired, Jesus, but the source of life gushed forth
for souls, and the ocean of mercy opened up for the
whole world. O Fount of Life, unfathomable Divine
Mercy, envelop the whole world and empty Yourself out
upon us.
(*Repeat the following prayer 3 times*) O Blood and
Water, which gushed forth from the Heart of Jesus as a
fountain of Mercy for us, I trust in You!

Our Father

Our Father who art in heaven, hallowed be Thy name;
Thy kingdom come; Thy will be done on earth as it is in
heaven. Give us this day our daily bread; and forgive us
our trespasses as we forgive those who trespass against
us. And lead us not into temptation; but deliver us from
evil. Amen.

Hail Mary

Hail, Mary, full of grace, the Lord is with thee. Blessed
art thou among women, and blessed is the fruit of thy
womb, Jesus. Holy Mary, Mother of God, pray for us
sinners, now and at the hour of our death. Amen.

The Apostles Creed

I believe in God, the Father Almighty, Creator of heaven and earth, and in Jesus Christ, His only Son, our Lord, who was conceived by the Holy Spirit, born of the Virgin Mary, suffered under Pontius Pilate, was crucified, died and was buried; He descended into hell; on the third day He rose again from the dead; He ascended into heaven, and is seated at the right hand of God the Father Almighty; from there He will come to judge the living and the dead. I believe in the Holy Spirit, the Holy Catholic Church, the communion of Saints, the forgiveness of sins, the resurrection of the body, and life everlasting. Amen.

The Eternal Father

Eternal Father, I offer You the Body and Blood, Soul and Divinity of Your dearly beloved Son, Our Lord Jesus Christ, in atonement for our sins and those of the whole world. Amen.

For the Sake of His Sorrowful Passion

For the sake of His sorrowful Passion, have mercy on us and on the whole world.

Concluding Doxology

Holy God, Holy Mighty One, Holy Immortal One, have mercy on us and on the whole world.

Closing Prayer

Eternal God, in Whom mercy is endless, and the treasury of compassion inexhaustible, look kindly upon us, and increase Your mercy in us, that in difficult moments, we might not despair, nor become despondent, but with great confidence, submit ourselves to Your holy will, which is Love and Mercy Itself. Amen.

Made in the USA
Columbia, SC
09 February 2021

31976117R00154